KNIT WITH BEADS

Beautiful Gifts

KNIT WITH BEADS

Beautiful Gifts

EASY TECHNIQUES • 18 UNIQUE DESIGNS

Scarlet Taylor

Project Photographs by Bill Milne

WATSON·GUPTILL PUBLICATIONS

New York

Executive Editor: JOY AQUILINO

Editor: ABIGAIL WILENTZ

Art Director: GABRIELE WILSON

Designer: JULIE DUQUET

Production Director: ALYN EVANS

Project photography: BILL MILNE

Step-by-step photography: DONALD SCOTT AND CONRAD LOWMAN

First published in 2007 by Watson-Guptill Publications,
Nielsen Business Media, a division of The Nielsen Company
770 Broadway, New York, NY 10003
www.watsonguptill.com

ISBN-10: 0-8230-1676-5
ISBN-13: 978-0-8230-1676-1

Library of Congress Control Number: 2007929718

Manufactured in China
First printing, 2007

1 2 3 4 5 6 7 8 9 / 15 14 13 12 11 10 09 08 07

DEDICATION AND ACKNOWLEDGMENTS

This, my second book, is dedicated to my second daughter, Katherine Taylor. With a special thank you for lending her time and talent to create the charts and schematics.

A special thank you to the following talented knitters for their hard work, dedication, and enthusiasm in creating the stunning projects for this book: Bobbie Anderson, Jan Ballew, Stella Bedard, Mary Elliott, Leah Galliker, Andrea Kelly, Marci (Posey) Salem, and Sally Wolford.

Thanks to Gina Allison and her staff at Caravan Beads in Wilmington, North Carolina, for their enthusiasm and inspiration, for allowing me to come into the store and "try on" beads, and for sharing their vast knowledge of beads with me.

Thanks to Conrad Lowman for his willingness to take on the job of Illustration photographer for this book, and for his attention to detail.

Thanks to Coy Taylor for the use of her hands and her patience in modeling the illustration photographs.

Thanks to Charlotte Quiggle for her thoroughness in editing these patterns, and for her dedication to this project.

Thanks to my editor, Joy Aquilino, for this incredible opportunity, and for her support and enthusiasm.

Thanks to graphic artist Natalie Fuechsel for her work on the charts and schematics.

And last but certainly not least, a special thanks to Phil, my husband and coach, for all he does to keep me inspired and sane!

CONTENTS

mindful of the fiber content of your yarn. I used elegant faux pearls for the Bridal Gauntlet and Garter set (see page 48) to go with the Muench Yarn Soft Kid mohair blend yarn. The delicate sheen of the pearls was the perfect complement to the soft "halo" of the fuzzy yarn.

Each of the projects in this book was designed with a specific yarn and bead in mind. Unique characteristics of the yarn—such as fiber content, twist, and weight—were considered in my choice of the right bead. Then I chose a beading technique that would best contribute to the success of the project. For best results, I recommend you use the yarn suggested in the pattern.

If you need to make a yarn substitution, be sure to follow the suggestions made above. If possible, before purchasing beads, try them on the yarn you prefer for a good fit. As with any knitting project, take the time to knit a swatch in the pattern stitch. Use whatever needle size you need to obtain the specified gauge.

Pre-Stringing Beads

There are beading needles and beading threads made specifically for beading purposes. For pre-stringing beads, I like to use a "big-eye" needle.

Where a pattern instructs you to pre-string beads, the number of beads given is the approximate number necessary for working the bead pattern while

1. The big-eye needle is made up of very thin, flexible wire that separates at the center, forming the "eye." Thread the yarn through the eye (above left) and secure at one end, leaving a short tail.

2. Thread each bead onto the needle at the opposite end, pushing the beads down the needle, then down the yarn (above). Tip: Don't try to thread too many beads before pushing them down the yarn. If there happens to be a bead with a smaller hole that doesn't want to fit, you'll have to remove all the beads to discard that one.

3. To prevent excessive wear on the yarn, unwind a generous length of yarn from your ball and push the beads down in small groups. Wind the yarn back into a ball, leaving a few beads close to the end so that they are available as you need them (left).

knitting with the first ball of yarn. If you find you need a few more beads as you near the end of the ball, don't cut your yarn—simply thread the additional beads from the tail end. If you have a few beads left over, just slide them off the yarn. Thread each additional ball of yarn with beads as needed to complete the pattern.

The total number of beads given in the materials list for each project is the approximate number of beads needed to complete the entire project—plus a few more to compensate for beads that are unusable. Often when you buy beads, some will be either broken or have holes that are not completely drilled out. Just discard those beads, or save them for other projects.

Things You Should Know

Instructions for many of the knitting techniques you'll need to complete these projects can be found in the Glossary of Terms and Techniques (page 100). Following the glossary is the Knitting Abbreviations list, which includes standard knitting abbreviations as well as special ones used in this book.

Instructions given for the beading techniques are for knitting flat (back and forth in rows) unless otherwise stated.

Blocking and Laundering

For knitted fabrics with beads, it's best to use a wet blocking technique, as most beads will not hold up well to steam or direct heat from pressing with an iron. I've found that lightly spraying the finished piece with cool water, blotting out the excess water with a clean white towel, then pinning the piece on a blocking surface to dry works very well.

Extra care should be taken in laundering your beaded knits. It's best to hand-wash the garment as you would your other delicate hand knits, taking special care of the beads. You may want to ask your bead supplier for advice on laundering specific types of beads you are purchasing. If the yarn label suggests dry cleaning, be sure to advise your dry cleaner not to steam or otherwise stress the beads.

Skill Levels

The skill levels described for each project in this book reflect the standards provided by the Craft Yarn Council of America:

Beginner: Projects use basic knit and purl stitches, for first-time knitters. Minimal shaping is involved.

Easy: These projects use basic stitches, repetitive stitch patterns, and simple color changes, and involve simple shaping and finishing.

Intermediate: Projects use a variety of stitches, such as basic cables and lace, simple intarsia, double-pointed needles, and knitting-in-the-round needle techniques, with mid-level shaping and finishing.

Experienced: These projects involve intricate stitch patterns, techniques, and dimension, such as non-repeating patterns, multicolored techniques, fine threads, small hooks, detailed shaping, and refined finishing.

Slip-Stitch Beaded Knitting

If you love slip-stitch knitting as much as I do, you'll really love this technique.

When you slip a stitch with the yarn in front of your work, you are left with that little strand of yarn that "floats" in front of the stitch that was slipped. What a perfect place for a bead . . . or two or three!

In slip-stitch beaded knitting, the beads are pre-strung, making it easy to slide a bead right up in front of a slipped stitch. Pay attention to your tension as you take the yarn back to the wrong side of your work and knit the next stitch. You want to be firm enough to hold the bead in place neatly, but you don't want the strand to be so tight that the fabric puckers.

Slip-stitch beaded knitting can be worked from either the right side or the wrong side. See the Ladies' Beaded Sock pattern (pages 30–35) for step-by-step instructions for slip sitch beaded knitting from the wrong side.

In the charts for patterns using this technique (i.e., where the bead sits in front of a slipped stitch), the bead is drawn within the square representing the stitch. You should slip the stitch as indicated by the pattern or chart.

TECHNIQUE

1. With pre-strung yarn, work across the row to the desired bead position indicated in the pattern by SBU. Bring the yarn forward to the right side (RS) of your work (wyif) between the two needles. Slip the next stitch (purlwise) from the left-hand needle to the right-hand needle.

2. Slide one bead up close to the right-hand needle, placing it in front of the slipped stitch. Keeping the bead in front (RS) of the work, bring the yarn to the back (WS) again to knit. Knit the next stitch as usual.

Sample fabric knit with slip-stitch beaded knitting.

Coy's Felted Clutch

Knit and felt with beads? Absolutely! Just follow the easy tips on page 19 for beautiful and successful results.

My oldest teenage daughter was the inspiration for this darling felted and beaded clutch. It's a perfect project for a beginner new to the "knitting scene." She made hers in less than a day! She always receives compliments from friends when she carries it.

SKILL LEVEL
Beginner

APPROXIMATE FINISHED MEASUREMENTS
Before Felting
Approx 12½ x 6" (with side seams sewn and flap folded closed, ready for felting)

After Felting
Approx 10½ x 4½" (with flap folded closed). *Size will vary depending on yarn used and amount of felting.*

MATERIALS
- Plymouth Galway Chunky (100% wool, 123 yds/113m, 3.5 oz/100 g): 2 skeins #141 fuchsia (for clutch)
- 1 skein each Plymouth Galway Worsted (100% wool, 210 yds/192 m, 3.5 oz/100 g) #137 yellow and #146 lime green (for felted rosettes and leaves)
- Approx 160 glass pebble beads #05161 from Mill Hill Beads/Wichelt Imports
- Size 13 (9 mm) knitting needles, or size needed to obtain gauge
- Size 11 (8 mm) knitting needles
- Size 11 (8 mm) double-pointed needles
- Bead stringing needle
- Tapestry needle

GAUGE
Before Felting
With larger needles in St st, 12 sts and 17 rows = 4"/10 cm.
After Felting
Approx 14 sts and 22 rows = 4"/10 cm.
To save time, take time to check gauge.

PATTERN STITCHES
Bead Pattern (mult of 4 sts + 1)
Row 1 (RS): K1, *k1, sl 1 wyif SBU, k2; rep from * across row.
Row 2 and all WS rows: Purl.
Row 3: Knit.
Row 5: K1, *k3, sl 1 wyif SBU; rep from * to last 4 sts, k4.
Row 7: Knit.
Row 8: Purl.
Rep Rows 1–8 for pat.

Stockinette Stitch (St st)
Knit on RS rows, purl on WS rows.

Garter St
Knit every row.

SPECIAL ABBREVIATION
SBU = Slide one bead up to the RH needle into position indicated by pat.

PATTERN NOTES
- Clutch is made in one piece, then folded envelope style for front, back, and flap.
- Gauge is not critical for working Rosettes and Leaves.

INSTRUCTIONS

Pre-string approx 111 beads.

With smaller needles, cast on 37 sts.

Knit 2 rows.

Next Row (RS): Change to larger needles, and beg with Row 1, work 6 reps (48 rows) of bead pat, then work Row 1 once more to end bead pat. Piece will measure approx 12".

FLAP
Next Row (WS): K2, work in St st (no beads) to last 2 sts, k2.

Cont in pat as est, maintaining first and last 2 sts in garter st for side edges until flap measures approx 3½" (14 rows), ending with a WS row.

Change to smaller needles and work beaded border for flap:

Next Row (RS): K1, *k1, sl 1 wyif SBU; rep from * to last 2 sts, k2. Knit 3 rows. Bind off all sts loosely.

WRIST STRAP
Pre-string approx 9 beads.

With double-pointed needles, cast on 3 sts. Work a beaded I-cord as follows:

Rows 1, 2, 3, and 4: Knit. Slip sts to end of needle.

Row 5: K1, sl 1 wyif SBU, k1. Slip sts to end of needle.

Rep Rows 1–5 until I-cord measures approx 9¾" from beg. Bind off.

FINISHING
With WS facing, fold bottom 6" up to RS and sew sides tog to form front and back of clutch, leaving top 4¼" unsewn for flap. Sew each end of wrist strap to inside of clutch at side seam. Weave in yarn ends.

FELTED ROSETTES (MAKE 4)
With larger needles and yellow, cast on 30 sts.

K1, *k2, bind off one st (2 sts on needle), [k1, bind off 1] 3 times; rep from * to end.

Cut yarn and thread through rem sts, pulling tightly. Secure and weave in yarn ends.

LEAVES (MAKE 6)
With larger needles and green, cast on 7 sts.

Row 10: Sl 1, purl to 6 sts past marker, p2tog, p1, turn.

Row 11: Sl 1, knit to 7 sts past marker, ssk, k1, turn.

Row 12: Sl 1, purl to 7 sts past marker, p2tog, p1, turn.

Row 13: Sl 1, knit to 8 sts past marker, ssk, k1, turn.

Row 14: Sl 1, purl to 8 sts past marker, p2tog, p1, turn.

Row 15: Sl 1, knit to 9 sts past marker, ssk, k1, turn.

Row 16: Sl 1, purl to 9 sts past marker, p2tog, p1, turn.

Row 17: Sl 1, knit to 10 sts past marker, ssk, turn.

Row 18: Sl 1, purl to 10 sts past marker, p2 tog, turn.

Row 19: Sl 1, k21. Cut D.

With B, pre-string approx 42 beads.

GUSSET

With B and RS facing, using same needle (now needle 1) pick up and knit 14 sts along side of heel flap. With a free needle (needle 2) knit 20 instep sts from each of next 2 needles. With another free needle (needle 3), pick up and knit 14 sts along other edge of heel flap, then with the same needle, knit 11 of heel sts, ending at marker. Needle 1 has 25 sts, needle 2 has 40 sts, needle 3 has 25 sts—90 sts.

CUFF BORDER

CHART A

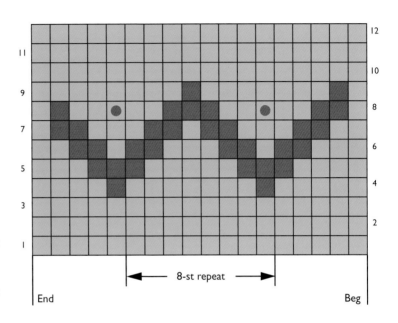

8-st repeat

End   Beg

COLOR KEY

□ = A

▢ = B

▨ = C

▨ = D

■ = E

STITCH KEY

□ = Knit on RS, purl on WS

⦿ = Bobble: Knit into front, back, front, back and front of next st (5 sts made from 1 st), turn; p5, turn; k2tog-tbl, k3tog, pass k2tog over k3tog

◉ = SBU, slip stitch wyif

FOOT

Keep marker in place for beg of rnd, and knit 1 rnd.

Next Rnd (Dec): Needle 1: Knit to last 3 sts, k2tog, k1; needle 2: knit; needle 3: k1, ssk, knit to end.

Rep Dec rnd [every third rnd] 4 times more—80 sts.

Number of sts is now the same as beg of heel: 40 sts on needle 2 and 20 sts each needles 1 and 3.

Cont even until foot measures approx 8" from beg of heel turn AND AT THE SAME TIME referring to photo or as desired, and using slip-stitch bead method same as for leg, randomly place beaded snowflakes from Chart B over last 20 sts of needle 2 and first 10 sts of needle 3 (same side of stocking as snow-man). Cut B.

TOE

Next Rnd (Dec): Needle 1: With D, knit to last 3 sts, k2tog, k1; needle 2: k1, ssk, knit to last 3 sts, k2tog, k1; needle 3: k1, ssk, knit to end.

Rep Dec rnd [every other rnd] 4 times, then [every rnd] 10 times. Needles 1 and 3 now have 5 sts each, needle 2 has 10 sts—20 sts.

Cut yarn, run tail through rem sts, and secure on WS.

FINISHING

Sew side (leg) seam.

Fold hem to inside of stocking at turning ridge and sew in place.

Embroider in black: small bullions (see Glossary, page 105) for snow-man's eyes, larger bullions for "buttons," and outline st for mouth. In red, make small bullion for nose.

With dpns and C, cast on 3 sts. Make a 2½" length of I-cord for hanging loop as follows: *k3, do not turn, but slide sts to end of needle; rep from *. Bind off. Sew ends tog, then attach to inside of stocking at side seam.

With B, make a 2" pom-pom (see Glossary, page 107) and attach to toe bind-off.

Weave in yarn ends.

Lightly wet-block stocking, avoid-ing beads.

Ladies' Beaded Socks

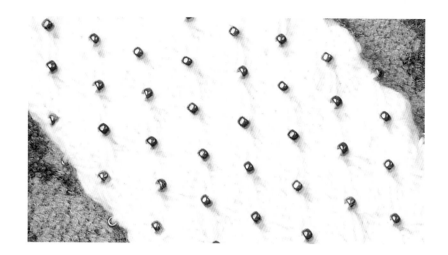

Here's the perfect sock to show off with your favorite clogs or "Birks."

Although it may look complicated, the stitch pattern really is easy. And being a slip-stitch pattern, it's perfect for adding just a few beads. In the previous slip-stitch beaded patterns, you worked the slipped stitch and the bead on the right side (RS) of your work. The technique is the same here, except the slipped stitch is worked from the wrong side (WS), so the yarn is held at the back (right side) of your work to add the bead. See page 32 for step-by-step instructions.

TECHNIQUE
Slip-Stitch Beaded Knitting on the Wrong Side

1. Work across the row to the desired bead position, indicated in the pattern by SBU, take the yarn back to the right side (RS) of your work (wyib) between the two needles.

2. Slip the next stitch(es) from the left-hand needle to the right-hand needle as instructed.

3. Slide one bead up close to the right-hand needle, placing it in front of the slipped stitch(es). Keeping bead on the RS, bring the yarn forward between the needles to the (WS) again to purl. Purl the next stitch as usual. You'll need to pay attention to your tension as you bring the yarn to the wrong side of your work and purl the next stitch. You want to be firm enough to hold the bead in place neatly, but you don't want the strand to be so tight that the fabric puckers.

Sample fabric knit with Slip-Stitch Beaded Knitting.

Intermediate

FINISHED SIZE
Women's average foot (wide foot)

MATERIALS
- Lorna's Laces Shepherd Sport (100% super-wash wool, 200 yds/183 m, 2.5 oz/70 g) 1 (2) skeins natural
- Approx 125 (135) size 6/0 Japanese seed beads. Sample knit with #6-462 metallic gold iris, from Caravan Beads.
- One each size 4 (3.5 mm) knitting needles and set of double-pointed (dpns) needles, or size needed to obtain gauge
- Beading needle
- 1 stitch marker
- Tapestry needle

GAUGE
In Beaded St pat 32 sts and 48 rows = 4"/10 cm.
In St st 24 sts and 32 rows = 4"/10 cm.
To save time, take time to check gauge.

PATTERN STITCHES
Beaded English Diamond Quilting (mult of 6 sts + 2)
Row 1 (WS): P1, *yo, p5, yo, p1; rep from *, ending row p1.
Row 2: K1, *sl 1 wyib, drop yo off needle, k4, sl 1 wyib, drop yo; rep from * across, ending row k1.
Row 3: P1, sl 1 wyib SBU, *p4, sl 2 wyib SBU; rep from * across to last 6 sts, p4, sl 1 wyif, p1.
Row 4: K1, *sl 1 wyib, k4, sl 1 wyib; rep from * across, ending row k1.
Row 5: P1, sl 1 wyif, *p4, sl 2 wyif; rep from * across to last 6 sts, p4, sl 1 wyif, p1.
Row 6: K1, *drop next st to front of work, k2, pick up dropped st and knit it; sl 2 wyib, drop next st to front of work, sl same 2 sts back to left-hand needle, pick up dropped st and knit it, k2; rep from * across ending row k1.
Row 7: P1, *p2, (yo, p1) twice, p2; rep from * across, ending row p1.
Row 8: K1, *k2, (sl 1 wyib, drop yo) twice, k2; rep from * across, ending row k1.
Row 9: P1, *p2, sl 2 wyib SBU, p2; rep from * across, ending row p1.

Row 10: K1, *k2, sl 2 wyib, k2; rep from * across, ending row k1.
Row 11: P1, *p2, sl 2 wyif, p2; rep from * across, ending row p1.
Row 12: K1, * sl 2 wyib, drop next st to front of work, sl same 2 sts back to left-hand needle, pick up dropped st and knit it; k2, drop next st to front of work, k2, pick up dropped st and knit it; rep from * across, ending row k1.
Repeat Rows 1–12 for pat.

K1, P1 Rib (over an even number of sts)
Row 1 (RS): *K1, p1 across row.
Rep Row 1 for pat.

SPECIAL ABBREVIATION
SBU = Slide one bead up to the RH needle into position indicated by pat.

PATTERN NOTES
- The cuff and leg sections of the socks are knit back and forth in rows, then stitches are divided onto double-pointed needles to work heel, then joined to complete the foot in the round.
- It's important to cast on loosely for a comfortable fit. Use a larger needle size if necessary.

INSTRUCTIONS

CUFF
Pre-string 110 (120) beads.

With knitting needles, loosely cast on 68 (74) sts.

Next Row (RS): Work in k1, p1 rib for approx 2", ending with a RS row.

LEG
Next Row (WS): Beg with Row 1, work even in Beaded English Diamond Quilting pat until piece measures approx 7" from beg, ending with Row 12 of pat.

Next Row (WS):
SMALL SIZE
[K2tog, k2] twice, [k2tog, k3, k2tog, k2] 6 times, k2tog, k2, ssk—52 sts.

LARGE SIZE
K2tog, k4, [k2tog, k3, k2tog, k4] 6 times, ssk—60 sts.

ALL SIZES
DIVIDE AND JOIN FOR HEEL
Distribute sts among 3 dpns as follows: With first dpn, k13 (15) sts, sl next 13 (15) sts onto 2nd dpn, sl next 13 (15) sts onto 3rd dpn, sl rem 13 (15) sts onto end of first dpn. There is now 1 needle with 26 (30) sts (heel) and 2 needles with 13 (15) sts each (instep).

HEEL
Heel flap is worked back and forth in rows with instep sts kept waiting on dpns as placed.

Next Row (WS): P26 (30), turn.

Row 1: *Sl 1 purlwise wyib, k1; rep from * to end.

Row 2: Sl 1 purlwise wyif, purl to end.

Rep Rows 1 and 2 until heel flap meas approx 2½" from beg, ending with a WS row.

HEEL TURN
Row 1 (RS): Sl 1, k12 (14), pm, k2, ssk, k1, turn.

Row 2: Sl 1, purl to 2 sts past marker, p2tog, p1, turn.

Row 3: Sl 1, knit to 3 sts past marker, ssk, k1, turn.

Row 4: Sl 1, purl to 3 sts past marker, p2tog, p1, turn.

Row 5: Sl 1, knit to 4 sts past marker, ssk, k1, turn.

Row 6: Sl 1, purl to 4 sts past marker, p2tog, p1, turn.

Row 7: Sl 1, knit to 5 sts past marker, ssk, k1, turn.

Row 8: Sl 1, purl to 5 sts past marker, p2tog, p1, turn.

Row 9: Sl 1, knit to 6 sts past marker, ssk, k1, turn.

Row 10: Sl 1, purl to 6 sts past marker, p2tog, p1, turn.

FOR LARGER SIZE ONLY
Row 11: Sl 1, knit to 7 sts past marker, k2tog, k1, turn.

Row 12: Sl 1, purl to 7 sts past marker, p2tog, p1, turn.

ALL SIZES
Last Row: Sl 1, k7 (8), pm, k8 (9).

GUSSET

With RS facing, using same needle (now needle 1), pick up and knit 15 sts along side of heel flap. With a free needle (needle 2), k13 (15) instep sts from each of next 2 needles. With another free needle (needle 3), pick up and knit 15 sts along other edge of heel flap, then with the same needle, k8 (9) heel sts,

ending at marker. Needle 1 has 23 (24) sts, needle 2 has 26 (30) sts, needle 3 has 23 (24) sts—72 (78) sts.

Keep marker in place for beg of rnd, and work 1 rnd even.

Rnd 1 (Dec): Needle 1: Knit to last 3 sts, k2tog, k1; needle 2: knit; needle 3: k1, ssk, knit to end.

Rnd 2: Knit around.

Rep Rnds 1 and 2, nine (eight) times more—52 (60) sts.

FOOT

Division of sts among needles is now the same as beg of heel: 26 (30) sts on needle 2 and 13 (15) sts each on needles 1 and 3.

Cont even until foot measures approx 2¼" less than desired finished length from beg of heel turn. (If unsure, compare piece to a sock that you own for best fit.)

TOE

Rnd 1 (Dec Rnd): Needle 1: Knit to last 3 sts, k2tog, k1; needle 2: k1, ssk, knit to last 3 sts, k2tog, k1; needle 3: k1, ssk, knit to end.

Rnd 2: Work even.

Rep Rnds 1 and 2 seven times more, then work only Rnd 1 twice.

Needles #1 and #3 now have 3 (5) sts, needle #2 has 6 (10) sts—12 (20) sts. With needle #3, work to end of sts on needle #1. You now have 2 needles, each with 6 (10) sts.

FINISHING

Graft toe tog with Kitchener st as follows:

Thread a tapestry needle with a 16" strand of yarn. Hold the 2 knitting needles parallel to each other with WS tog, using tapestry needle, join as follows:

Pass needle through first stitch on front needle as if to purl. Leave stitch on needle.

Pass needle through first stitch on back needle as if to knit. Leave stitch on needle.

*Pass needle through first stitch on front needle as if to knit, then through next stitch on needle as if to purl. Drop first stitch on front needle off.

Pass needle through first stitch on back needle as if to purl, then through next stitch on needle as if to knit. Drop first stitch on back needle off*.

Rep from * to * until there is only one stitch on each needle.

Pass needle through rem stitch on front needle as if to knit and drop stitch off.

Pass needle through rem stitch on back needle as if to purl and drop stitch off. Fasten off by weaving in the yarn end.

Knitting with Beads in Garter Stitch

This is one of the easiest methods for knitting with beads. And it's fun!

Although beads are added to Garter stitch on a wrong-side (WS) row, the beads fall to the right side (RS) of your work. All you need to do is slide a bead up close to your needle and then knit the next stitch. The bead will sit in front of and between two stitches. Watch your tension so that the bead stays firmly in place against the fabric. You don't want it to be "droopy" or so tight that the fabric puckers.

In the charts for patterns using this technique (that is, where the bead sits between two stitches), the bead is drawn on the vertical line in the graph between two stitch squares. You should work the first stitch as indicated in the chart (in this case, knit), slide the bead up, then work the next stitch as indicated (also knit when working Garter stitch).

TECHNIQUE

With pre-strung yarn, knit across the row to the desired bead position indicated in the pattern or chart by SBU. Keep the yarn at the back (WS) of your work in knit position, slide one bead up close to the needle, then knit the next stitch as usual. The bead then sits on the strand between two knit stitches on the right side. Make sure the bead doesn't droop on the strand. It should rest nicely against the fabric.

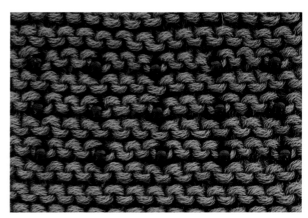

Sample fabric knit with beads in Garter stitch.

Urban Camo Bag

Bags for men are all the rage. From messenger to diaper, men are discovering what women have known all along—you gotta have a great bag to carry all your stuff!

Check out this bag for your favorite guy…or gal. It's knit with a trendy camouflage yarn in a mixture of textures with wooden beads.

My husband and youngest daughter, Katie, having just been on a hiking trip, came up with the idea of these unique strap closures made from carabiners to give the bag a rugged look.

For added stability, I used Lorna Miser's easy technique for fusing lining to knit bags. It's from her leaflet *Knit & Fused Purses* (see Bibliography).

It's an easy-to-knit pattern and is easy to knit with beads. Combine two methods of knitting with beads: knit the beads in garter stitch along the bottom front edge and use the slip-stitch method for the star emblem.

SKILL LEVEL
Easy (Basic sewing skills helpful)

FINISHED MEASUREMENTS
Approx 12" x 12½" x 2½"

MATERIALS
- Bernat Camouflage (100% acrylic, 195 yds/175 m, 3.5 oz/100 g) 3 skeins #10483 renegade
- Approx 125 size 5 mm round brown wooden beads
- Size 6 (4.25 mm) knitting needles, or size needed to obtain gauge
- Size 8 (5 mm) knitting needles, or size needed to obtain gauge
- Beading needle
- 4 stitch markers
- Tapestry needle
- 2 approx 2¼" carabiner clips (key-chain type) (optional; see Pattern Notes)
- 2 approx 3" carabiner clips
- Approx 45" of 2" wide black webbing
- Approx 12" of ½" wide black webbing (optional; see Pattern Notes)
- Approx 1½ yd Therm O Web HeatnBond UltraHold Iron-On Adhesive
- Approx 1 yd of 44" wide black fabric for lining

GAUGE
With smaller needles in Garter st, 18 sts and 36 rows = 4"/10 cm.
With larger needles in St st, 18 sts and 24 rows = 4"/10 cm.
To save time, take time to check gauge.

PATTERN STITCHES
Beaded Border (mult of 2 sts)
Row 1 (WS): K2, *SBU, k2; rep from * across row.
Row 2 and 4 (RS): Knit.
Row 3: Knit.
Rep Rows 1–4 for pat.

Stockinette Stitch (St st)
Knit on RS rows, purl on WS rows.

Garter Stitch
Knit every row.

SPECIAL ABBREVIATION
SBU = Slide one bead up to the RH needle into position indicated by pat.

PATTERN NOTES
- If you would rather not cut and sew the ½" straps for the front closures, look for carabiner key chains with a black strap already attached. I found mine at my local home improvement store. They are inexpensive, so I purchased 4, giving me the 4½" straps needed for the closures.
- Bag front and back are constructed in 1 piece, beginning at top front and ending with flap. Side gussets are picked up and worked separately, then joined to sides of bag.

··

INSTRUCTIONS

With smaller needles, cast on 54 sts.

Work in Garter st until piece measures approx 1" from beg, ending with a WS row.

Change to larger needles, and beg St st with a RS row. Work even until piece measures approx 10" from beg, ending with a RS row.

Cut yarn and pre-string 78 beads.

Rejoin yarn to WS row and change to smaller needles.

Work 2 rows in Garter st.

Beg with Row 1, work 2 repeats of Beaded Border pat, then work Row 1 once more.

Work 2 rows in Garter st.
Change to larger needles, and

work even in St st until piece measures approx 12½" from beg, ending with a WS row.

Next Row (RS): Purl across for turning ridge.

Cont in St st until piece measures approx 2½" from turning ridge for bottom, ending with a WS row.

Next Row (RS): Purl across for turning ridge.

Cont in St st until piece measures approx 27½" from beg, ending with a RS row.

BEADED STAR

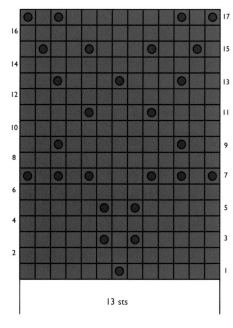

13 sts

KEY
▇ = Knit on RS, purl on WS

◉ = SBU, slip stitch wyif

FLAP

Next Row (WS): K4, pm, purl across row to last 4 sts and inc 1 st in center st, pm, k4—55 sts.

Cont in pats as est, maintaining first and last 4 sts in Garter st for side borders throughout, for approx 6" (if you don't plan to line your bag, work for approx 3"), ending with a WS row.

Cut yarn and pre-string 26 beads.

Next Row (RS): Rejoin yarn and work across first 21 sts, pm, work Row 1 of Beaded Star Chart, pm, work across rem 21 sts.

Cont in pats as est, working Beaded Star pat between markers, until last row of chart has been completed. Remove markers.

Work in St st for approx 1¼" from end of Star pat, ending with a RS row.

Change to smaller needles, and work in Garter st for approx 1", ending with a WS row. Bind off loosely.

SIDE GUSSETS

With larger needles and RS facing, pick up and k 14 sts between markers on one side of 2" bottom. Work even in St st until gusset measures approx 14" from beg, ending with a WS row. Bind off.

Rep for second side of bag.

FINISHING

Block edges of bag flat from WS. Trace bag measurements onto paper side of iron-on adhesive. Following manufacturer's instructions, fuse iron-on adhesive to wrong side of lining. Cut out fabric using pinking shears. Peel off paper and pin WS of knit bag to fusible side of fabric, being careful to align bag and lining edges so that lining does not show. Fuse to fabric with adhesive side on WS of fabric.

Sew side gussets to front and back on each side. Fold top approx 1½" of each side gusset to WS of bag, insert larger carabiner, and sew in place for strap.

SHOULDER STRAP

Turn each end of 2" webbing under and sew a 1½" seam for carabiner hem. Attach larger carabiners.

FRONT STRAPS

(if making straps for front closures) Cut 4 pieces of ½" webbing to 3". For each strap, turn ends under and sew ½" seam. Attach 2 straps to each small carabiner, sliding one around to each end. Center straps on either side of star and sew loose ends of straps to flap and bag leaving enough slack to open clip.

4

Knitting with Beads Between Purl Stitches

If you can purl, you can knit with beads using this technique. It's that easy!

With this technique, the bead sits on the strand and is held in place between two purl stitches on either side. You'll want to make sure the strand isn't too loose or the bead will look "droopy" and be prone to snagging. On the other hand, you don't want to pull too tightly, because that will cause the fabric to pucker under the bead. Practice on your gauge swatch, and you'll get it in no time at all.

In the charts for patterns using this technique (that is, where the bead sits between two stitches), the bead is drawn on the vertical line in the graph between two stitch squares. Work the first stitch as indicated in the chart (in this case, purl), slide the bead up, then work the next stitch as indicated (also purl).

TECHNIQUE

<table>
<tr>
<td>

1. With pre-strung yarn, work across the right-side (RS) row to within one stitch of the desired bead position indicated in the pattern or chart by SBU. Purl the next stitch.

</td>
<td>

2. Then, with the yarn still in front of your work, slide one bead up close to the needle and purl the next stitch. The bead then sits on the strand and is held in place between two purl stitches on the right side. Make sure the bead doesn't "droop" on the strand. It should rest nicely against the fabric.

</td>
</tr>
</table>

Sample fabric knit with beads between purl stitches.

Quiggle Neckwarmer

This is a really fun design for knitting with beads. And unique! It's knit with a bulky, thick-and-thin yarn, pre-strung with beads. Not at all common for most knitting with beads methods.

I found these unusual size 2/0 beads at my local bead store. Larger than any other glass seed bead I've seen, I knew they would be perfect to use with a novelty yarn.

In experimenting with colors, my bead supplier and I liked the look of mixed colored beads on this variegated yarn. If you prefer, use one or even more colors.

Knitting with beads between two purl stitches is a clever way to add beads to this K2, P2 Rib pattern worked in the round to the collar, then worked flat for a comfortable shawl collar.

FINISHED MEASUREMENTS
Circumference: Approx 24½" worked to approx 19" at neck edge.
Length: 10"

MATERIALS
- Berroco Hip-Hop (100% wool, 76 yds/70 m, 3.5 oz/100 g): 2 hanks # 7236 Be-Bop
- Approx 150 size 2/0 Japanese seed beads. Sample knit with Magic Royal Mix from Caravan Beads
- Size 10 (6 mm) 24" circular knitting needle
- Size 11 (8 mm) 24" circular knitting needle
- Size 13 (9 mm) 24" circular knitting needle, or size needed to obtain gauge
- Stitch marker
- Bead stringing needle
- Tapestry needle

GAUGE
With size 13 needles in K2, P2 Rib, 13.5 sts = 4"/10 cm unstretched.
To save time, take time to check gauge.

PATTERN STITCHES
Circular K2, P2 Beaded Rib (for body) (multiple of 8 sts)
Rnd 1: *K2, p2; rep from * around.
Rnd 2: *K2, p1 SBU p1, k2, p2; rep from * around.
Rnds 3, 4 and 5: Work same as Rnd 1.
Rnd 6: *K2, p2, k2, p1 SBU p1; rep from * around.
Rnds 7 and 8: Work same as Rnd 1.
Rep Rnds 1–8 for pat.

K2, P2 Beaded Rib (for collar)
Row 1 (WS): *P1 SBU p1, k2; rep from * across.
Rows 2, 3, and 4: *P2, k2; rep from * across.
Rep Rows 1–4 for pat.

SPECIAL ABBREVIATION
SBU = Slide one bead up to the RH needle into position indicated by pat.

PATTERN NOTE
Work the body portion of the neckwarmer in the round, then turn and work the collar back and forth in rows.

INSTRUCTIONS

BODY
Pre-string approx 50 beads.

Beg at lower edge with size 13 circular needle, loosely cast on 80 sts. Join, being careful not to twist sts, and pm for beg of rnd.

Work in Circular Beaded K2, P2 Rib pat until piece measures approx 1¼" from beg.

Change to size 11 needle, and cont in pat as est until piece measures approx 3½" from beg.

Change to size 10 needles, and cont in pat as est until piece measures approx 7" from beg.

Turn and work collar back and forth in rows:

Next Row (WS): Work Row 1 of Beaded K2, P2 Rib for collar.

Cont in pat as est, and work 2 reps of pat, then work Row 1 once more.

Work one row even, then bind off loosely in pat.

FINISHING
Weave in yarn ends. Fold collar over allowing beads to show on public side.

TECHNIQUE

Although these 2/0 beads fit nicely on this thick-and-thin yarn, it's a little more difficult to thread them over a double thickness of the "thicker" slubs of yarn. Thread the beading needle with the thinner part of the yarn, allowing the bead to easily pass over.

Bridal Gauntlets and Garter

For a truly exquisite (and unique) gift for the bride-to-be, make this bridal set featuring pearl-embellished ivory gauntlets and garter. They are reminiscent of Lady Guinevere and the romance of Camelot.

The main stitch pattern is easy-to-knit Garter stitch, which works up quickly in the round. The beaded ruching pattern adds interest even a more experienced knitter will appreciate. Ruching is a technique that adds bands of gathers to the fabric. It's done simply by increasing the number of stitches being worked and changing to a larger needle size. Then, to complete the ruching effect, decrease back to the original number of stitches and needle size. Simple, yet so beautiful! Especially with the addition of beads.

I used faux pearls for these sample pieces. If you prefer to use freshwater or other pearls, be sure to check the size and shape of the drill holes for pre-stringing.

SIZE
Woman's Average

FINISHED MEASUREMENTS
Gauntlets
Circumference: Approx 8"
Length: 8½"

Garter
Circumference: Approx 15" at
3" above knee.

MATERIALS
- Muench Yarns/GGH Yarns Wollywasch (100% superwash pure wool, 137 yds/125 m, 1.75 oz/50 g): 1 ball #23 ivory (A)
- Muench Yarns/GGH Yarns Soft-Kid (70% super kid mohair, 25% nylon, 5% new wool, 150 yds/138 m, 1 oz/25 g): 1 ball # 001 ivory (B)
- Approx 400 size 4 mm simulated pearl beads. Sample knit with #'77724 from Bead Heaven
- Size 4 (3.5 mm) set double-pointed knitting needles
- Size 5 (3.75 mm) set double-pointed knitting needles
- Size 6 (4.25 mm) set double-pointed knitting needles, or size needed to obtain gauge
- Stitch marker
- Bead stringing needle
- Approx 16" length of ½" non-roll elastic
- Approx 10" length of ¼" ivory satin ribbon
- Optional: white elastic thread
- Safety pin
- Sharp sewing needle and ivory thread
- Tapestry needle

GAUGE
With size 5 needles in Garter st,
21sts and 48 rows = 4"/10cm.
To save time, take time to check gauge.

PATTERN STITCHES
Circular Garter st
Rnd 1: Purl around.
Rnd 2: Knit around.
Rep Rnds 1 and 2 for pat.

Circular Stockinette st (St st)
Knit every rnd.

SPECIAL ABBREVIATION
SBU = Slide 1 bead up to the RH needle into position indicated by pat.

PATTERN NOTE
To avoid damage to the delicate mohair yarn, pre-string only the number of beads needed for each bead row. The rows are few and far between, so it doesn't take too much time or create too many yarn ends to weave in.

INSTRUCTIONS
Gauntlets
RIGHT HAND
With size 5 needles and A, loosely cast on 42 sts. Divide evenly among 3 dpns and join, being careful not to twist sts, and pm for beg of rnd.

GARTER ST BAND
*Work in Garter st for approx 1". Cut A.

With B, pre-string 21 beads.

RUCHING BAND
Next Rnd (Inc): Join B, and knit into the front and back of every stitch— 84 sts.

Change to size 6 needles and work Bead Rnd as follows:

Bead Rnd: K1, *p1 SBU p1, k2; rep from * around to last 3 sts; p1 SBU p1, k1.

Cont even in St st until band measures approx 1" from Garter st band. Cut B, and pre-string 21 beads.

Next Rnd: Re-join B and rep Bead Rnd.

Next Rnd (Dec): K2tog around— 42 sts.

Change to size 5 needles and A.* Rep from * to * 1 time. Change to size 4 needles, and rep from * to * once more, working garter band with size 4 needles and ruching band with size 6 needles.

With size 4 needles, cont even in Garter st for approx 1".

THUMB OPENING
Next Rnd: K28, bind off next 8 sts, k6.

Next Rnd: Cast on 8 sts over bound-off sts from previous rnd. Cont in Garter st for approx 1". Pre-string 21 sts.

Next Rnd: *P1 SBU p1; rep from * around. Bind off loosely.

Work left hand same as for right hand, reversing thumb opening as follows: K6, bind off next 8 sts, k28. Cont as for right hand.

FINISHING
Weave in yarn ends. Optional: For a tighter fit, pass 3 rows of elastic thread through WS of arm edge (first garter band). Secure ends together.

Garter

With size 5 needles and A, loosely cast on 78 sts. Divide evenly among 3 dpns and join, being careful not to twist sts, and pm for beg of rnd.

Work in Garter st for approx 1¾". Cut A.

With B, pre-string 26 beads.

Next Rnd (Inc): Join B, and knit into the front and back of every st—156 sts.

Bead Rnd 1: *K4, p1 SBU p1; rep from * around.

Work 4 rnds in St st. Cut B, pre-string 26 beads.

Bead Rnd 2: *K1, p1 SBU p1, k3; rep from * around.

Change to size 6 dpns, and work in St st for 4 more rnds. Cut B, pre-string 26 beads.

Rep Bead Rnd 1.

Next Rnd: Knit around.

Next Rnd: Purl around.

Next Rnd: Bind off knitwise.

FINISHING

Fold Garter st band in half to WS for elastic casing and sew hem, leaving last 2" open. Attach safety pin to one end of elastic and draw it through the casing. Overlap ends of elastic and sew. Finish sewing hem. Weave in yarn ends.

Tie a small bow from ribbon and sew to center front. Trim to desired length. Embellish with a small beaded daisy. (See Technique below.)

TECHNIQUE
Beaded Daisy

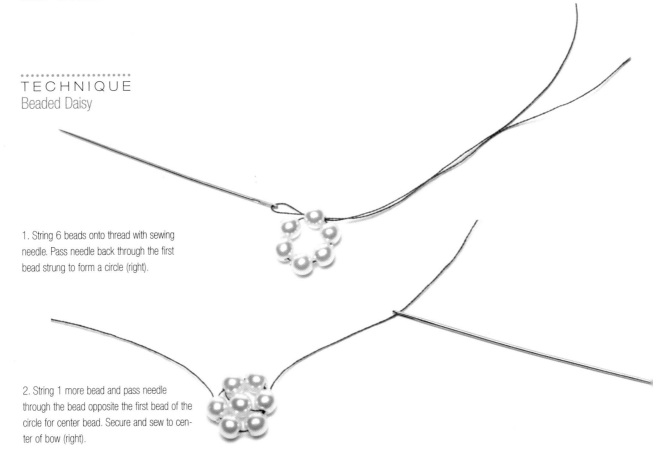

1. String 6 beads onto thread with sewing needle. Pass needle back through the first bead strung to form a circle (right).

2. String 1 more bead and pass needle through the bead opposite the first bead of the circle for center bead. Secure and sew to center of bow (right).

Beaded Cables Scarf, Mittens, and Hat Set

We already know that cables totally impress our "non-knitting" friends, right? But cables and beads? WOW! And it's just as easy to add the beads as it is to knit the cables.

Cables are like a frame for beads, with the bead "mounted" right in the center of the crossings. Because most simple cables are worked over an even number of stitches, you'll need to add the bead between the two center stitches. Knitting with beads between purl stitches works great, and the purl stitches are hidden within the cable. For the bead to be in the center of the cable, the center row needs to be a right-side row. Therefore you need to cross the cable on Row 4, 8, 12, and so on.

SCARF

FINISHED MEASUREMENTS
Approx 7" x 64" (excluding fringes)

MATERIALS
- Classic Elite Yarns Skye Tweed (100% wool, 110 yds/105.5m, 1.75 oz/150 g): 5 skeins #1253 tapestry
- Approx 275 size 6/0 Japanese seed beads. Sample knit with #6-151 cobalt from Caravan Beads.
- Size 7 (4.5 mm) circular knitting needles, or size needed to obtain gauge
- Cable needle
- Bead stringing needle
- 6 stitch markers
- Tapestry needle

GAUGE
In Beaded Cable and Rib Pat, 28 sts and 21 rows = 4"/10 cm.
To save time, take time to check gauge.

PATTERN STITCHES
Beaded Cables
See Charts A and B.

P2, K2 Rib (multiple of 4 sts)
Row 1: P2, k2.
Row 2: Purl the purl sts and knit the knit sts.
Rep Row 2 for pat.

SPECIAL ABBREVIATION
SBU = Slide 1 bead up to the RH needle into position indicated by pat.

INSTRUCTIONS

Pre-string approx 62 beads.

Cast on 48 sts.

SET UP RIB PATS AND CHART B
Next Row (RS): P2, k2, pm, work Row 1 of Chart B over next 8 sts, pm, [k2, p2] twice, pm, work Row 1 of Chart B over next 8 sts, pm, [p2, k2] twice, pm, work Row 1 of Chart B over next 8 sts, pm, k2, p2.

Cont in rib and cable pats as est, and work 2 reps of Chart B.

SET UP CHART A
Next Row (RS): Cont in pats as est to 2nd marker; work Row 1 of Chart A over next 24 sts, removing 3rd and 4th markers, cont in pats as est to end of row.

Pattern is now set up as follows: P2, K2 Rib, marker, Chart B, marker, Chart A, marker, Chart B, marker, K2, P2 Rib.

Cont in pats as est until scarf measures approx 62" from beg, ending with Row 24 of Chart A.

SET UP RIB PATS AND
CHART B TO COMPLETE
Next Row (RS): Cont in pats as est to 2nd marker, [k2, p2] twice, pm, work Row 1 of Chart B over next 8 sts, pm, [p2, k2] twice, cont in pats as est to end of row.

Cont in pats as est, and work 2 reps of Chart B.
Bind off loosely in pat.

Weave in yarn ends.

FRINGE
For each fringe, cut 6 strands of yarn, each 14" long. Fold strands in half, insert crochet hook from back to front through stitch, and pull fold through to back. Pull ends through fold—pull tightly. Evenly fringe along cast on and bind off edges. Trim fringe edges neatly to desired length.

CHART A

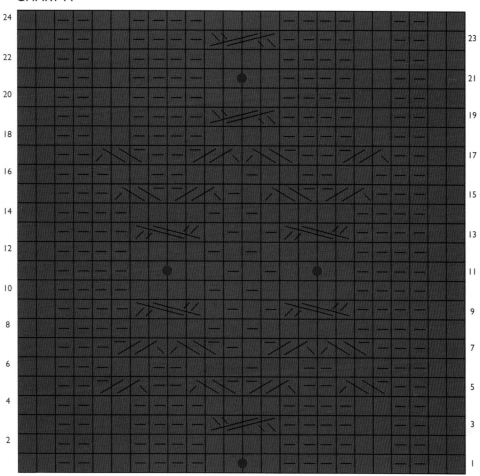

CHART B

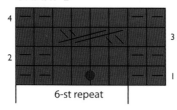

6-st repeat

KEY

▓	= Knit on RS, purl on WS
▭	= Purl on RS, knit on WS
●	= SBU between 2 purl sts
▧	= Slip 2 sts to cn and hold in back, k2, k2 from cn
▧	= Slip 2 sts to cn and hold in front, k2, k2 from cn
▧	= Slip 1 st to cn and hold in back, k2, p1 from cn
▧	= Slip 2 sts to cn and hold in front, p1, k2 from cn

MITTENS

FINISHED MEASUREMENTS
Length from wrist to fingertips: 10"
Wrist circumference: 6½"
Hand circumference: 8"

MATERIALS
- Classic Elite Yarns Skye Tweed (100% wool, 110 yds/105.5 m, 1.75 oz/150 g): 1 skein #1253 tapestry
- Approx 60 size 6/0 Japanese seed beads. Sample knit with #6-151 cobalt from Caravan Beads.
- Size 5 (3.75 mm) knitting needles
- Size 7 (4.5 mm) knitting needles, or size needed to obtain gauge
- Cable needle
- Bead stringing needle
- 3 stitch markers
- Stitch holder
- Tapestry needle

GAUGE
With larger needles in Beaded Cables Pat, 24 sts and 26 rows = 4"/10 cm.
With larger needles in St st, 16 sts and 24 rows = 4"/10cm.
To save time, take time to check gauge.

PATTERN STITCHES
K1, P1 Rib (multiple of 2 sts)
Row 1 (RS): *K1, p1: rep from * across.
Rep Row 1 for pat.

Beaded Cables (multiple of 6 sts + 2)
See Chart B.

Stockinette Stitch (St st)
Knit on RS rows, purl on WS rows.

SPECIAL ABBREVIATIONS
SBU = Slide 1 bead up to the RH needle into position indicated by pat.

INSTRUCTIONS

RIGHT MITTEN

CUFF
Pre-string approx 24 beads.

With smaller needles, loosely cast on 38 sts.

Work in K1, P1 Rib pat for approx ¾", ending with a WS row.

SET UP PATS
Next Row (RS): Change to larger needles, P2, *k4, p2; rep from * across row.

Next Row: Beg with Row 2, work 4 reps of Beaded Cables pat, then work Row 1 once more. Cuff should measure approx 3¼".

HAND
Next Row (Dec) (WS): K8, [k2tog, k8] 3 times—35 sts.

Beg with a RS row, work 4 rows even in St st.

BEG THUMB INCREASES
Row 1 (RS): K16; pm for thumb, M1, k1, M1, pm; k16—37 sts.

Row 2: Purl.

Rep Rows 1 and 2 until there are 13 sts between markers for thumb.

Next Row (RS): K16, place the 13 thumb sts onto stitch holder, k16.

Cont even on these 34 sts for hand until mitten measures approx 8½" from beg of cuff, ending with a WS row; on last row, place a marker at center of row between first and last 17 sts.

TOP SHAPING
Row 1 (RS): K1, ssk, knit to within 2 sts of marker, k2tog, slip marker, ssk, knit to last 3 sts, k2tog, k1—30 sts.

Row 2 (WS): P1, p2tog, purl to within 2 sts of marker, ssp, slip marker, p2tog, purl to last 3 sts, ssp, p1—26 sts.

Rep Rows 1 and 2 five times more—6 sts rem.

Next Row (WS): Purl.

Cut yarn, leaving 6" tail. Run tail through rem sts, and secure.

THUMB

With RS facing, return 13 sts from holder to needle. Join yarn and cont even in St st until thumb measures approx 2¼" from beg, ending with a WS row.

Next Row: K2tog across, ending k1—7 sts.

Next Row: P2tog across, ending p1—4 sts.

Cut yarn, leaving a 6" tail. Run tail through rem sts, and secure.

LEFT MITTEN

Work same as for Right Mitten.

FINISHING

Sew mitten and thumb side seams. Weave in yarn ends.

HAT

FINISHED MEASUREMENTS
Circumference: 21"
Depth: 8"

MATERIALS
- Classic Elite Yarns Skye Tweed (100% wool, 110 yds/105.5 m, 1.75 oz/50 g): 2 skeins #1253 tapestry
- Approx 150 size 6/0 Japanese seed beads. Sample knit with #6-151 cobalt from Caravan Beads
- Size 5 (3.75 mm) knitting needles
- Size 7 (4.5 mm) knitting needles, or size needed to obtain gauge
- Cable needle
- Bead stringing needle
- 3 stitch markers
- Tapestry needle

GAUGE
With larger needles in Beaded Cables pat, 24 sts and 26 rows = 4"/10 cm.
With larger needles in St st, 16 sts and 24 rows = 4"/10 cm.
To save time, take time to check gauge.

PATTERN STITCHES
K1, P1 Rib (mult of 2 sts)
Row 1 (RS): *K1, p1: rep from * across.
Rep Row 1 for pat.

Beaded Cables (mult of 6 sts + 2)
See Chart B.

Stockinette Stitch (St st)
Knit on RS rows, purl on WS rows.

SPECIAL ABBREVIATIONS
SBU = Slide one bead up to the RH needle into position indicated by pat.

INSTRUCTIONS

CUFF

Pre-string approx 126 beads.

With smaller needles, loosely cast on 128 sts.

Work in K1, P1 Rib pat for approx ¼", ending with a WS row.

Setup Row (RS): Change to larger needles. P2, *k4, p2; rep from * across row.

Next Row: Beg with Row 2, work Beaded Cables pat from chart until cuff measures approx 4½" from beg, ending with Row 1 of chart.

Next Row (WS): K1, [k2tog, k1] 42 times, k1—86 sts.

SHAPE TOP AND CROWN

Beg with a RS row, work 2 rows even in St st.

Next Row (RS): K1, [k2tog, k24, ssk, pm] 3 times, k1—80 sts.

Next Row and All WS Rows: Purl.

Next Row: K1, [k2tog, knit to 2 sts before marker, ssk] 3 times, end k1—74 sts.

Rep last 2 rows until 14 sts rem.

Cut yarn, run tail through rem sts, pull tightly, and secure on WS.

Sew seam. Weave in yarn ends.

5 Knitting with Beads Through a Stitch

Knitting with beads through a stitch is often referred to as Beaded Knitting. Beads are pre-strung onto the working yarn as in the previous technique, but the beads are actually slipped into a stitch, rather than between or in front of stitches. You can "knit" the bead through as you are knitting a stitch or "purl" the bead through as you are purling a stitch.

Occasionally a bead will have a mind of its own and want to slide down the "leg" of the stitch, through the center of the stitch below, landing on the strand between two stitches. If that happens, gently guide it back into place. However, if it happens more than occasionally, it's probably because the bead is too small for the knitting. Try using a bead that is a little larger or, if gauge is not critical, a smaller size needle so the center of the stitch is a bit smaller.

TECHNIQUE

1. With pre-strung yarn, work across the row to the desired bead position indicated in the pattern or chart by BK1. Insert the knitting needle into the stitch to be knit as usual.

2. With the yarn at the back (WS) of the work, slide one bead up close to the needle, and knit both the yarn and the bead through the stitch. A little nudge with the left index finger helps to push the bead through the stitch.

3. To keep the bead stable, on the following row, purl the stitch that the bead is on through the back loop, making sure the bead is on the right side (RS) of the fabric. Tip: Insert the needle into the stitch above the bead to ensure the bead falls to the front (RS) of the work.

Sample fabric knit with beads through a knit stitch.

Kids' Beaded Socks

Kids especially love the bright colors of today's popular clogs and sandals. These fun pony beads are just *too cute* for a pair of kid's beaded socks. Be advised, however, that the manufacturer recommends this bead for ages 6 and up, so the pattern is sized accordingly.

The socks are made in the round, meaning you are always working on the right side (RS). Therefore, instead of purling the beaded stitch through the back loop (tbl) on the following row, you'll knit it through the back loop (k1-tbl) on the following round (rnd). It's easy and fun knitting.

The beads are "stacked" by color in this pattern. Therefore, they have to be strung in reverse order. In other words, you will string the beads for the last bead round of the pattern first and the beads for the first bead round last. The last beads strung are the first to be knitted off the strand. Or, you be the designer! Design your own color pattern or just grab a handful of beads and start stringing! You'll get a fun, confetti-mix look.

FINISHED SIZE
Child's Average, Age 6–12
Circumference: Approx 6½"
Length: Approx 6½–7"

MATERIALS
- Classic Elite Flash (100% mercerized cotton, 93 yds/85 m, 1.75 oz/50 g) 1 skein #6102 spring valley
- 1 package size 5 mm multicolor pony beads (readily available at craft stores)
- One size 6 (4.25 mm) set of 5 double-pointed knitting needles
- One size 7 (4.5 mm) set of 5 double-pointed knitting needles, or size needed to obtain gauge
- Beading needle
- Stitch marker
- Tapestry needle

GAUGE
With larger needles in St st, 20 sts and 24 rnds = 4"/10 cm.
To save time, take time to check gauge.

PATTERN STITCHES
Beaded K1, P1 Rib (multiple of 4 sts)
Rnd 1: *K1, p1, BK1, p1; rep from * around.
Rnd 2: *K1, p1, k1-tbl, p1; rep from * around.
Rnd 3: Work same as Rnd 1.
Rnd 4: Work same as Rnd 2.
Rnd 5: *BK1, p1, k1, p1; rep from * around.
Rnd 6: *K1-tbl, p1, k1, p1: rep from * around
Rnd 7: Work same as Rnd 5.
Rnd 8: Work same as Rnd 6.

Circular Stockinette St (St st)
Knit every rnd.

SPECIAL ABBREVIATIONS
BK1 = Knit 1 bead through a knit st.

PATTERN NOTE
It's important to cast on loosely for a comfortable fit. Use a larger needle size if necessary.

INSTRUCTIONS

CUFF
Pre-string 32 beads in this order (or as desired):

Fourth rnd of beads: orange, red, dk blue, yellow, lavender, pink, white, lt blue

Third rnd of beads: same as last

Second rnd of beads: lt blue, yellow, dk blue, white, red, pink, orange, lavender

First rnd of beads: same as second

Loosely cast on 32 sts.

Distribute evenly on 4 smaller dpns, join without twisting, and pm for beg of rnd.

Work Rnds 1–8 of Beaded K1, P1 Rib pat.

Change to larger needles, and work 3 rows in St st.

DIVIDE FOR HEEL
Redistribute sts for heel as follows: K8, then slip 8 sts from last needle of rnd to other end of first needle. There is now 1 needle with 16 sts (heel) and 2 needles with 8 sts each (instep).

HEEL
Heel flap is worked back and forth in rows with instep sts reserved on dpns as placed.

Next Row (WS): Purl across, turn.

Row 1: *Sl 1 purlwise wyib, k1; rep from * to end.

Row 2: Sl 1 purlwise wyif, purl to end. Rep Rows 1 and 2 until heel flap measures approx 1½" from beg, ending with a WS row.

HEEL TURN
Row 1 (RS): K8, pm, k2, ssk, k1, turn.

Row 2: Sl 1, purl to 2 sts past marker, p2tog, p1, turn.

Row 3: Sl 1, knit to 3 sts past marker, ssk, k1, turn.

Row 4: Sl 1, purl to 3 sts past marker, p2tog, p1, turn.

Row 5: Sl 1, knit to 4 sts past marker, ssk, turn.

Row 6: Sl 1, purl to 4 sts past marker, p2tog, turn.

Last Row: Sl 1, knit rem 9 sts.

GUSSET
With RS facing, using same needle (now needle 1), pick up and knit 7 sts along side of heel flap; needles 2 and 3: knit across instep sts.; needle 4: pick up and knit 7 sts along other edge of heel flap, then with the same needle, knit 5 heel sts from needle 1, ending at marker. Needles 1 and 4 have 12 sts each; needles 2 and 3 have 8 sts each—40 sts.

Keep marker in place for beg of rnd, and work 1 rnd even.

Rnd 1 (Dec): Needle 1: knit to last 3 sts, k2tog, k1; needles 2 and 3: knit; needle 4: k1, ssk, knit to end—38 sts.

Rnd 2: Knit around.

Rep Rnds 1 and 2 two times more, then work Rnd 1 once more—32 sts, 8 on each needle.

FOOT

Cont even until foot measures approx 4 to 4½" from beg of heel turn (or 2½" less than desired finished length). If unsure, compare piece to a sock that you own for best fit.

TOE

Rnd 1 (Dec Rnd): *Needle 1: Knit to last 3 sts, k2tog, k1; needle 2: k1, ssk, knit to end; rep from * across needles 3 and 4—28 sts.

Rnd 2: Work even.

Rep Rnds 1 and 2 five times more—8 sts.

FINISHING

Cut yarn, leaving a 6" tail. Using tapestry needle, thread tail through rem stitches, pull tightly, and fasten off by weaving in the yarn end.

Weave in cast on end.

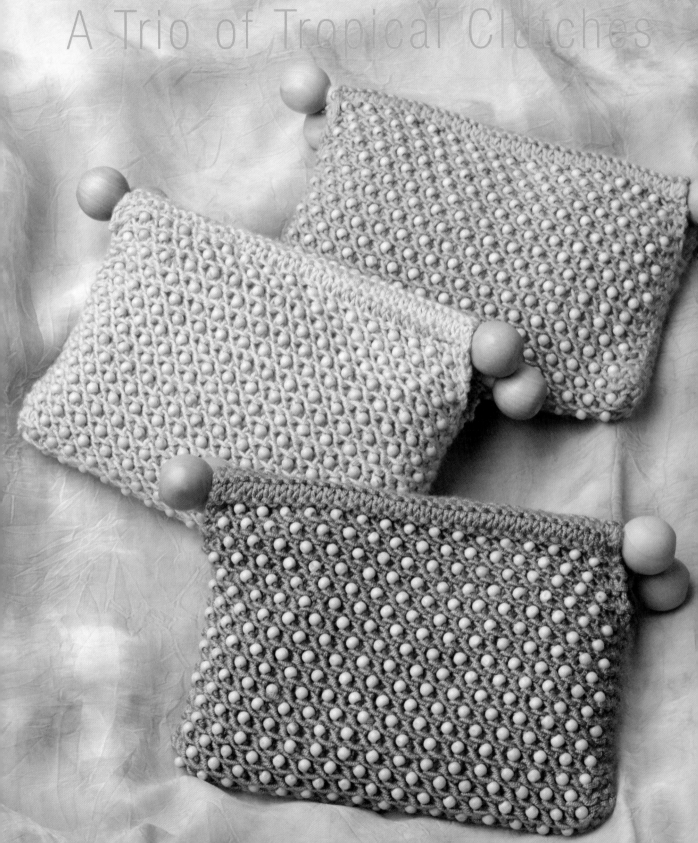

A Trio of Tropical Clutches

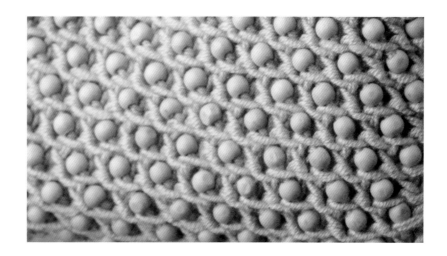

This is such a fun little stitch pattern to work, and so pretty with the addition of beads. You'll want to make all three! The twist? A twisted drop stitch. And a slight twist in the technique for knitting with beads through a knit stitch. With this pattern, the bead is knit through the stitch on the WS rather than the RS. See page 68 for step-by-step instructions.

Knitting with Beads Through a Knit Stitch…with a Twist!

1. Work to the desired bead location indicated in the pattern as BK1. Insert knitting needle into the stitch to be knitted as usual, wrap the yarn around both needles once, then around the RH needle once more.

2. Slide one bead up close to the needle and work both the yarn and the bead through the stitch.

3. A little nudge with the left index finger helps to push the bead through the stitch. Allow the bead to fall to the back (RS) of your work. On the following row, making sure the bead is facing you (RS), dropping the extra wraps, knit the stitch that the bead is on through the back loop. Tip: Hold the bead with your left thumbnail as you knit the stitch to be sure it stays on the RS.

SKILL LEVEL
Intermediate

FINISHED MEASUREMENTS
Approx 7" x 5"

MATERIALS
- Lion Brand Microspun (100% microfiber acrylic, 168 yds/154 m, 2.5 oz/70 g) 1 skein for each clutch, shown in #194 lime, #186 mango, and #148 turquoise
- Approx 570 size 5 mm round natural wooden beads for each clutch
- Size 6 (4.25 mm) knitting needles, or size needed to obtain gauge
- Size 4 (3.5 mm) knitting needles
- Beading needle
- Tapestry needle
- ¼ yd cotton lining fabric for each clutch
- Two ⅜" wooden dowels (at least 8" long) and two 1" dowel caps to make 2 rod type handles for each clutch. Both readily available at your local craft store.
- Wood glue

GAUGE
With larger needles, in St st pat, 20 sts and 25 rows = 4"/10 cm.
To save time, take time to check gauge.

PATTERN STITCHES
Beaded Twisted Drop St (over an even number of sts)

Row 1 (WS): K2, *BK1 wrapping yarn around both needles, then around RH needle once more, k1 wrapping yarn in same manner (every st is twisted, every other st is beaded); rep from * across row to last 2 sts, k2.

Row 2: K2, *dropping the extra wraps, k1, k1-tbl (stitch with bead); rep from * across row to last 2 sts, k2.

Row 3: K2, *k1 wrapping yarn around both needles, then around RH needle once more, BK1 wrapping yarn in same manner; rep from * across row to last 2 sts, k2.

Row 4: K2, *dropping the extra wraps, k1-tbl (stitch with bead); k1, rep from * across row to last 2 sts, k2.

Garter Stitch
Knit every row.

SPECIAL ABBREVIATIONS
BK1 = Knit 1 bead through a knit st.

PATTERN NOTE
Clutch front and back are constructed in 1 piece, then folded in half and joined with side seams.

INSTRUCTIONS

With your choice of color, pre-string approx half of the total number of beads, or fewer if you prefer. You can cut the yarn, string additional beads as needed, then reattach the yarn.

With smaller needles, cast on 36 sts.

HEM (FOR HANDLE)
Next Row (RS): Work even in Garter st until piece measures approx 1½" from beg, ending with a RS row.

Next Row: Change to larger needles, and work even in Beaded Twisted Drop St pat until piece measures approx 11½" from beg, ending with Row 1 of pat.

HEM (FOR HANDLE)
Next Row: Change to smaller needles, and work even in Garter st for approx 1½", ending with a WS row. Bind off.

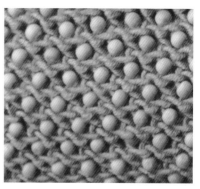

FINISHING

Fold clutch in half (lengthwise) and sew sides tog, leaving top 1" of st pattern and hems unsewn, to allow clutch to open. Fold half of each hem toward the inside (WS) of clutch and sew in place.

To line clutch, cut fabric 7⅓" x 10½". Fold in half with RS tog and sew sides tog with a ¼" seam. Turn bag inside out and whip stitch lining to bag just below Garter st hem and along open sides.

HANDLES

For each clutch, cut 2 wooden dowels to 8 inches in length. Insert dowel through hem and attach caps with wood glue. *Optional: Before attaching caps, spray with a little clear enamel spray to protect from dirt and oils.

Bead Knitting

Think of those beautiful Victorian beaded bags our great-grandmothers were so fond of. In true Bead Knitting, a bead is worked through every stitch and row of a motif or pattern so that you don't see any fabric, just beads. It's beautiful, but very time-consuming, and is the most difficult of all the beading techniques.

As with knitting with beads through a knit stitch, the bead is worked through the stitch (either knit or purled). However, if worked as an all-over design, the fabric will have a tendency to bias.

To avoid this problem, work the design in Plaited Stitch. Doing so will help secure the bead on the leg of the stitch as well. It's a fun stitch pattern and easy to work.

In the charts for patterns using this technique (i.e. where the bead is worked through a stitch), the bead is drawn within the square representing the stitch. You should work the bead along with the stitch as indicated by the chart (either knit or purled).

TECHNIQUE

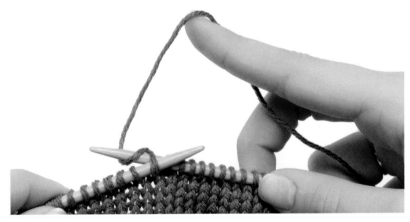

1. Working on RS rows with no beads, insert needle into the back of the stitch, wrap the yarn around the needle clockwise (going over RH needle rather than under it), and knit the stitch through the back loop.

2. Working on RS rows with beads, insert needle into the back of the stitch, BK1.

3. Wrap the yarn around the needle clockwise (going over RH needle rather than under it) and knit the bead and yarn through the back loop of the stitch.

4. Working on WS rows with beads, BP1, purling the stitch as normal. Working on WS rows with no beads, purl all stitches as normal.

Sample fabric knit with Bead Knitting.

Scented Sachets

Bead knitting can be a bit daunting at first. All those beads! And in every row! But it doesn't have to be. Just think small and simple. Projects like these cute little scented sachets are really quite fun to bead.

Instead of working an all-over beaded fabric, try this new technique for the first time by working a simple motif on a background of Plaited Stitch. You'll get the hang of the stitch pattern in no time at all.

Shiver me timbers! You'll be shocked at how easy Bead Knitting can be. Fill this Jolly Roger with a fetching fragrance for your pirate's treasure chest—or sock drawer—arrr! Fill the cupid's heart sachet with a delicate rose fragrance for a touch of romance.

And don't forget to personalize your gift by using one of the other techniques you've learned in this book. We added beaded fringe made from bone beads to the corners of the pirate's flag. You could use pink crystals to fringe all around the edges of cupid's heart.

FINISHED MEASUREMENTS
Approx 3" x 5"

MATERIALS
For Pirate's Flag Sachet
- Lion Brand Wool (100% wool, 158 yds/144 m, 3 oz/85 g): 1 skein each #153 ebony (A), and #099 winter white (B).
- Approx 125 size 6/0 Japanese seed beads. Sample knit with # 6-591 pearl Ceylon from Caravan Beads.
- Approx 16 asst mini round bone beads (readily available at craft stores)
- Size 8 (5 mm) knitting needles, or size needed to obtain gauge
- Bead stringing needle
- Beading or sewing needle
- Approx 2 oz of potpourri or fragrance beads to fill sachet. Sample filled with Dragon's Blood Fragrance Beads, available at discount department stores.
- Small amount of muslin for tie bags
- Tapestry needle

For Cupid's Heart Sachet
- Reynolds Signature (80% acrylic, 20% wool, 220 yds/201 m, 3.5 oz/100 g): 1 skein each #68 (A) red, and #84 (B) pink.
- Approx 75 size 6/0 Japanese seed beads. Sample knit with # 6-355 hot pink lined crystal AB from Caravan Beads.
- Size 8 (5 mm) knitting needles, or size needed to obtain gauge
- Bead stringing needle
- Approx 2 oz of potpourri or fragrance beads to fill sachet. Sample filled with rose water fragrance beads, available at discount department stores.
- Small amount of muslin for tie bag
- Tapestry needle

GAUGE
In Plaited st, with Lion Brand Lion yarn,18 sts and 25 rows = 4"/10 cm.
In Plaited st, with Reynolds Signature yarn, 17 sts and 28 rows = 4"/10 cm.
To save time, take time to check gauge.

PATTERN STITCHES
Plaited St
RS rows with no beads: Insert needle into the back of the stitch, wrap the yarn around the needle clockwise (going over RH needle rather than under it), and knit the stitch through the back loop.

RS rows with beads: Insert needle into the back of the stitch, wrap the yarn around the needle clockwise (going over RH needle rather than under it), and knit the bead and yarn through the back loop of the stitch.

WS rows with no beads: Purl as normal.

WS rows with beads: Purl the stitch as normal, pushing bead through the stitch.

Stockinette St (St st)
Knit on RS rows, purl on WS rows.

INSTRUCTIONS

PIRATE'S FLAG SACHET
With A, pre-string 100 beads.

Cast on 23 sts.

Beg with Row 1, and work Beaded Skull and Crossbones Pat from chart.

Next Row (RS): Purl across for turning ridge.

Change to B, beg St st, and work back of sachet to measure same as front from turning ridge.

Bind off.

CUPID'S HEART SACHET
With A, pre-string 75 beads.

Cast on 21 sts.

Beg with Row 1, and work Beaded Cupid's Heart Pat from chart.

Next Row (RS): Purl across for turning ridge.

Change to B, beg St st, and work back of sachet to measure same as front from turning ridge.

Bind off.

FINISHING
Fill muslin baggie with fragrance beads and secure with tie.

Fold sachet at turning ridge and sew one side tog and bottom seam. Place baggie inside sachet and sew rem side seam. Weave in yarn ends.

PIRATE'S FLAG FRINGES
Using black yarn and beading or sewing needle, string 4 beads for each fringe. Skip last bead strung, and thread needle back up through beads. Secure and sew fringe to corners of sachet.

BEADED SKULL AND CROSSBONES

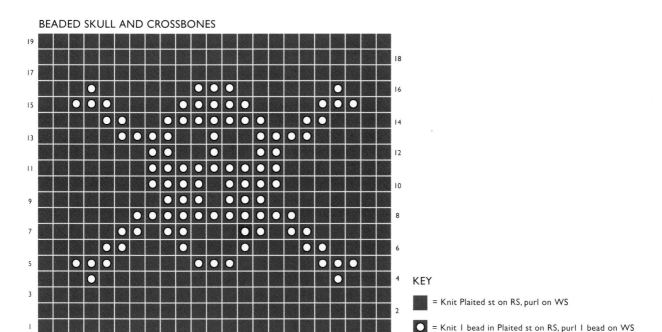

23 sts

KEY

■ = Knit Plaited st on RS, purl on WS

⊙ = Knit 1 bead in Plaited st on RS, purl 1 bead on WS

BEADED CUPID'S HEART

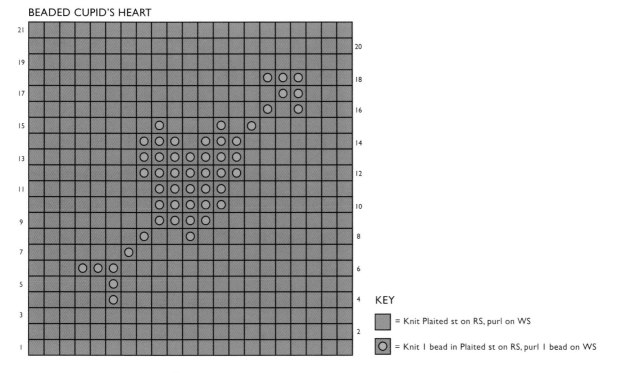

21 sts

KEY

▨ = Knit Plaited st on RS, purl on WS

◯ = Knit 1 bead in Plaited st on RS, purl 1 bead on WS

Hook Beading

There are times when pre-stringing beads is neither necessary nor practical. For instance, you may want to add just a sprinkling of beads to your knitting and question the need to pre-string just a few beads, constantly pushing them down the strand and out of your way. Or, if you are using a delicate yarn, the friction caused by sliding the beads will weaken or damage the strands. Perhaps you have chosen a bead that has a definite shape, such as a tulip or a heart, but the hole runs through the center of the bead from top to bottom rather than side to side. Of course, you would like the bead to sit upright on your knitting.

The way to knit in beads without pre-stringing is Hook Beading. It's done with a small crochet hook. In the charts for patterns using this technique (that is, where the bead is hooked onto the stitch), the bead is drawn within the square representing the stitch. Work the stitch as indicated in the chart after hooking the bead.

TECHNIQUE

1. Work across the row to the desired bead position indicated in the pattern or chart. First, with a crochet hook, hook the bead.

2. Then hook the next stitch from the left-hand needle.

3. Pull the stitch through the bead (above), return it to the left-hand needle, then either slip the stitch purlwise to the right-hand needle, or knit it as instructed by the pattern.

Sample fabric knit with Hook Beading.

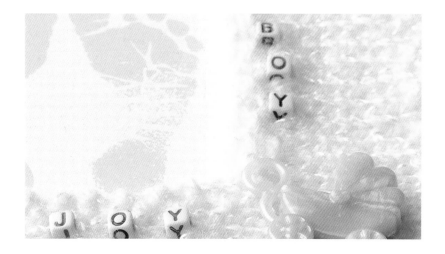

As a treasured gift for a special mom-to-be, present special moments from the baby shower in this precious little photo album with a knitted and beaded cover.

Boy or girl? Charts for both are included. For an added personal touch, collect a few party favors and ribbons from the shower to embellish your cover, making your gift a true keepsake of Mom's special event.

These little alphabet beads are so cute and really perfect for use in knitting with beads. The hole is drilled through the sides, so the letter will sit upright if you want to use a method that requires pre-stringing. Since they are being used here to outline the center photo area of the cover, however, I wanted them to be especially neat and straight. Hook beading worked the best, with just a few little nudges with my fingertips to keep the beads "in line." Knit the cover from side to side, hooking the beads right-side up, so the bead is facing you on the hook. It's easy and works the same whether you're working on a right-side (RS) or a wrong-side (WS) row.

MATERIALS
- Red Heart Baby Econo (90% acrylic, 10% polypropylene, 460 yds/421 m, 6 oz/170 g) 1 skein #1224 yellow
- 2 packages (104 pc pck) 5 mm asst. color pastel cube alpha beads (readily available at craft stores; see Pattern Note)
- Size 5 (3.75 mm) knitting needles
- Size 6 (4.25 mm) knitting needles, or size needed to obtain gauge
- Size 7 (1.5 mm) steel crochet hook
- 4 stitch markers
- Tapestry needle
- 6½" x 12¼" mini photo album (readily available at craft and discount department stores)

GAUGE
With larger needles in St st, 20 sts and 28 rows = 4"/10 cm.
To save time, take time to check gauge.

PATTERN STITCHES
Stockinette Stitch (St st)
Knit on RS rows, purl on WS rows.

Seed Stitch (over an odd number of sts)
Row 1: P1, *k1, p1; rep from * across row.
Rep Row 1 for pat.

PATTERN NOTE
For "girl" lettering, you may need only 1 package; purchase 2 to ensure you have the color mix desired.

INSTRUCTIONS

With smaller needles, cast on 81 sts.

Work 3 rows in Seed st.

Next Row (RS): Change to larger needles and cont in Seed st as est over first 3 sts, beg St st and knit across row to last 3 sts, cont Seed st over last 3 sts.

Work 7 more rows in pats as est, maintaining first and last 3 sts in Seed st throughout.

Next Row (RS): Work in pats as est across first 14 sts, pm, work Row 1 of Chart 1 over next 17 sts, pm, cont in pats as est to end of row.

Next Row: Cont in pats as est, working Row 2 of Chart 1 between markers.

Next Row: Work to first marker, work first 3 sts from Chart 1, join a second ball of yarn and bind off center 11 sts in Seed st, cont in pats as est to end of row.

Next Row (WS): Work to first marker, work Row 1 of Chart 2 over 3 sts; with second ball of yarn, work Row 1 of Chart 3 over 3 sts ending at second marker, work in pats as est to end of row.

Cont in pats as est, working both sides at once with separate balls of yarn, until Row 17 of Charts 2 and 3 have been completed.

Next Row (RS): Work Row 18 of Chart 3 and using Single cast-on method (see Glossary), cast on 11 sts over previously bound off sts, work in pats as est to end of row.

Next Row: Work to first marker, work Row 1 of Chart 4 (boy or girl) over 17 sts ending at second marker, work in pats as est to end of row.

Cont in pats as est until Chart 4 is completed.

Next Row (RS): Work in pats as est to first chart marker, remove and cont in St st to last chart marker, remove and work in pats as est to end of row.

Cont in pats as est, and work 8 more rows.

Change to smaller needles, and work in Seed st for 3 rows. Bind off.

FINISHING
Weave in yarn ends.

Center cover on photo album book as desired. Fold overlap on each end to fit album and sew sides to make flaps. Insert book ends into flaps. Trim a photo, invitation, or other memento from the event and place in "window" of cover, securing to album front with double-sided tape. Glue or sew keepsake party favors to cover. *Optional: If desired, further secure cover with a little fabric glue along the edges.

Chart 4

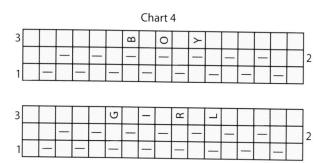

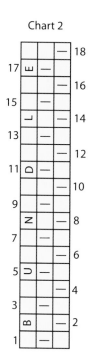

Chart 2

Chart 3

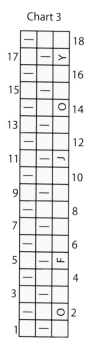

Chart 1

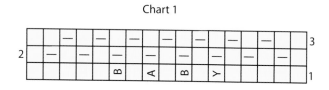

KEY

☐ = Knit on RS, purl on WS

— = Purl on RS, knit on WS

Knitting with Sequins

Shiny, shimmering, glittery sequins! Yes, you can even knit with sequins. In general, sequins are a little more challenging to work with than beads. The holes are smaller and the sequins are almost paper thin and usually larger than beads, making them a bit more difficult to slip through a stitch. As with beads, you need to pre-string sequins onto the yarn before beginning to knit. Given the tiny holes in most sequins, you are limited to very fine yarn. You might expand the range of yarn possibilities by using a second strand of very lightweight yarn (or thread) that you've pre-strung with the sequins; knit it in as you would when knitting with two strands held together.

Before you start to knit, string the sequins properly to ensure they lie correctly on the fabric; not doing so can alter the finished look of the piece. If the sequin is cupped, you should string the cupped side (which is faceted and reflects the most light) toward the skein so it faces outward once it is knitted into the fabric.

This book demonstrates three of several different methods for knitting with sequins—in this case, we're using ring-type sequins. Other methods may be used with different styles of sequins. Determining which method to use depends mostly on the sequin and the desired look of your finished project.

TECHNIQUE
Stringing Sequins

The ring-type sequins used for the project in this chapter are great to work with! The hole is larger than in a traditional sequin, so you are not as limited in choice of yarn, and you can see the hole much more easily. String these sequins so that the cupped side is facing the ball of yarn.

Sequins are a little more difficult to separate than beads. Slide a small group of sequins up at a time. Press the group flat against the strand of yarn with your thumb and forefinger, then use your thumbnail to separate one sequin from the group.

Knitting with Sequins Secured by a Purl Stitch

Working a purl stitch on one side of a sequin will secure the sequin on the right side (RS) and helps to hold the sequin flat against the fabric. With pre-strung yarn, work across the row to the stitch where the sequin is to be added. Bring the yarn forward between the needles to the right side (RS), slide one sequin up close to the work, and then purl the next stitch.

Knitting Sequins in Seed Stitch

With this method, the sequins are knit through the stitch, like knitting with beads through a knit stitch (see Chapter 5, page 60). Then, on following wrong-side (WS) rows, the sequins are held in place by purl "nubs." With pre-strung yarn, work across right-side (RS) rows (as indicated in pattern or chart by BK1), knitting every stitch; knit a sequin through every other stitch. On following wrong-side (WS) rows, purl the stitches as usual with sequins, and knit the stitches without.

Knitting with Sequins on a Carry-Along Thread

The bead or sequin pattern will determine how to carry along the thread. If you are working over a bead pattern in which the bead rows are close together, you can drop the carry-along and work the next wrong side row with the knitting yarn only, picking it up again for the next bead row. If the bead rows are farther apart, you can carry the thread along the side of the work, as you would when working small color change repeats, picking it up as needed to work a bead row. I like to use embroidery floss for this method. You can easily separate the strands, as you would for cross-stitch, using as few strands as necessary. It's available in hundreds of colors, too, making it easy to match almost any yarn color. You can use beading, sewing, or even crochet thread if you like. I have the most success using a cotton or wool thread that is not too silky or slippery, allowing it to hold on to the fibers of the yarn so it doesn't droop later.

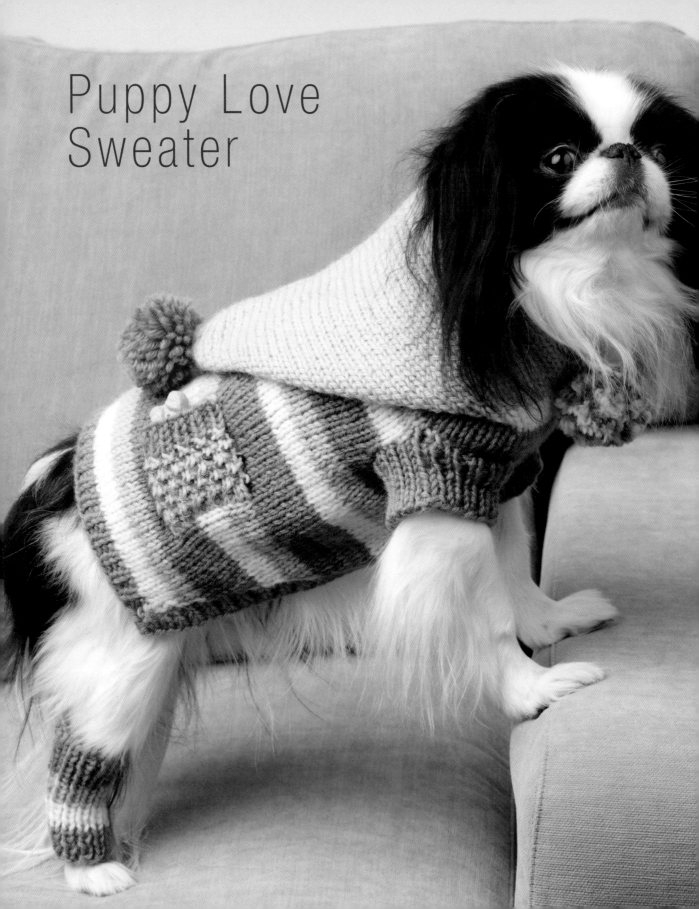

Puppy Love
Sweater

Give that doggie a bone—and a sweater! Tuck a treat in the pocket of this colorful hoodie made just for your little "puppy love." To add sparkle to your little one's walk in the park, knit in some shiny sequins. This pattern introduces three different methods for knitting with sequins.

You may actually pre-string ring sequins on worsted weight yarn. However, the yarn hides a bit more of the sequin than I would like. So for the hood section of the pattern where only a few sequins were added, I used a carry-along thread, pre-strung with the sequins, worked along with the main yarn. To knit in the sequins on the hood, use the method that secures the sequin with a purl stitch. (See instructions on preceding page.)

For the pocket, I used a Sequin Seed Stitch from June Hiatt's book, *The Principles of Knitting.* (See instructions on preceding page and in the pattern which follows.) Since there are many sequins (to add lots of "bling"), you can pre-string the sequins onto the working yarn to work using this method.

Intermediate

SIZE
Toy Breed

FINISHED MEASUREMENTS
Chest circumference: 14"
Length (back): 11"

MATERIALS
- Plymouth Galway (100% wool, 210 yds/192 m, 3.5 oz/100 g) 1 skein each #89 lavender (A), #1 white (B), #111 mint green (C) #129 blue (D)
- Approx 75 size 6 mm embossed iridescent ring sequins. Sample knit with #MTC81-55 dark orchard from Cartwright's Sequins
- Size 8 (5 mm) knitting needles or size needed to obtain gauge
- Size 7 (4.5 mm) knitting needles
- Size 6 (4.25 mm) knitting needles and set of double-pointed needles
- Bead stringing needle
- One skein DMC embroidery floss #598
- Stitch marker
- Tapestry needle

GAUGE
With larger needles in St st, 18 sts and 26 = 4"/10 cm.
To save time, take time to check gauge.

PATTERN STITCHES
Stripe Sequence (worked in St st over 16 rows)
Work *4 rows B, 4 rows C, 4 rows D, 4 rows A: rep from *.

Stockinette Stitch (St st)
Knit on RS rows, purl on WS rows.

K1, P1 Rib (over an even number of sts)
Row 1: *K1, p1; rep from * across row. /rnd.
Rep Row 1 for pat.

SPECIAL ABBREVIATIONS
SBU = Slide one bead (sequin for this project) up to the RH needle into position indicated in pat.

BK1 = Knit 1 bead (sequin for this project) through a stitch.

INSTRUCTIONS

With size 6 needles and A, cast on 40 sts.

Work in K1, P1 Rib for approx ½", ending with a WS row.

SHAPE BACK

Next Row: Change to size 8 needles, beg stripe sequence, and inc 1 st (M1) at beg and end of this row, then every 4th row 5 times, then every other row 6 times—64 sts.

Cont even until piece measures approx 7½" from beg, ending with last row of D in stripe sequence.

SHAPE LEG OPENINGS

Work both leg openings at the same time in Stripe sequence. Wind off small balls of yarn for each.

Next Row: K5, join a 2nd ball of yarn and bind off next 10 sts, k34, join a 3rd ball of yarn and bind off next 10 sts, knit rem sts—44 sts.

Work until leg openings measure approx 2" from beg, ending with a WS row.

Next Row (RS): Cast on 10 sts over bound-off sts for each leg opening—64 sts.

Cut yarn on 2nd and 3rd balls of yarn.

Cont even in pat for approx 2", ending with last row of B.

NECK AND HOOD

Join C and work 4 rows even.

Next Row (RS): Inc for hood: K5, M1, [k6, M1] 9 times, k5—74 sts.

Work even in C only until hood measures approx 6½" from beg, ending with a WS row. Bind off.

POCKET

With C, pre-string 30 sequins.

With size 8 needles, cast on 13 sts.

Beg St st and purl 1 row.

Row 1 (RS): K1, *BK1, k1; rep from * across row.

Row 2: P1, *p1, k1; rep from * to last 2 sts, p2.

Rep Rows 1 and 2 twice more (6 rows total).

Next Row (RS): Change to size 6 needles, and work in K1, P1 Rib for approx ½", ending with a WS row. Bind off in pat.

FINISHING

Sew chest seam from rear of leg shaping to hood.

BACK BAND

With size 6 needles and A, with RS facing, beg at lower edge and pick-up and k 36 sts evenly along right edge of back. Work in K1, P1 Rib for approx ½", ending with a WS row. Bind off in pat. Rep for left edge, beg at chest seam.

LEG BANDS

With dpn and A, pick up and k 40 sts evenly around leg opening. Join, and pm for beg of rnd. Work in K1, P1 Rib until band measures approx 1½" from beg. Bind off in pat. Rep for second leg opening.

SEQUINED HOOD TRIM

Fold hood in half and sew top seam.

Unwind a generous length (approx 50") of embroidery floss and separate the six strands so that you have 2 three-strand lengths.

Pre-string approx 15 sequins onto each length. Use a separate length for each of the 2 sequin rows.

With size 7 needles and A, pick up and k 62 sts evenly around hood. Beg St st and purl one row.

Work sequin pat as follows:

Row 1 (RS): With A and floss held tog, k2, *SBU p1, k3; rep from * across row.

Row 2: With A only, purl.

Row 3: With A and 2nd length of floss held tog, k1, *k3, SBU p1; rep from * across to last st, k1. Cont in A only for remainder of band.

Row 4: Purl.

Row 5: Knit.

Next Row (WS): Knit across for hem turning ridge.

Cont in St st until hem measures same as band from turning ridge. Bind off.

Whip st hem to WS.

TWISTED CORD AND POM-POMS

With 1 strand each of A, B, and C, make a 23" length of twisted cord. With 1 strand each of A, B, C, and D, make two 2" pom-poms for hood ties. With A, make one 2½" pom-pom for hood. Thread cord through hood hem and attach a pom-pom to each end. Attach pom-pom to point of hood. (See Glossary for detailed instructions for making twisted cord and pom-poms.)

Pin, then sew pocket in place approx 1½" from cast on edge and right-hand side.

OPTIONAL LEG WARMERS (MAKE 2)

The knitter of this cute little sweater thought Puppy needed leg warmers to keep the back legs warm, too!

With dpn and A, cast on 26 sts. Join, and pm for beg of rnd. Working in K1, P1 Rib, work 4 rnds each of A, B, C, D, then A again. Bind off in pat. Slip each warmer on back leg and fold over in a cuff as needed to adjust for fit.

Beaded Fringe

Add some "motion" to your knitting with beaded fringe! It's a fun adornment that will add a little "swish and sway" to any project. And it's a great opportunity to use some of those beautiful, tiny beads that you've had to pass over in the bead store because the holes were too small for pre-stringing.

You can use beads of the same size and color, or of several different sizes and colors to make up one fringe. Just keep the weight of the beads in mind so your fringes don't get too heavy. I like to use size 11/0 and 8/0 seed beads to make up the main fringe and size 3 mm and 4 mm rounds, drops, or shaped beads as accents and anchor beads. For a little inspiration to get you going on your own fringed designs, take a look at the bead combinations used on some of your favorite beaded jewelry.

TECHNIQUE

1. The bead at the bottom serves as the anchor bead that holds all the other beads in place. With beading needle and thread, string beads as instructed for one fringe. Skip the last bead strung (bead closest to the needle), and thread the needle back up through the remaining beads. Now you have one single strand of dangling beads forming one fringe. The bead at the bottom serves as the anchor bead that holds all the other beads in place.

2. To attach the fringe to your knitting, bring the needle up through the leg of a stitch from right to left, piercing each side of the stitch rather than coming up through the center (above). Make a small knot by drawing the needle through a loop, tightening the tension between the beads just enough so that none of the thread shows through. Don't let them get too tight though, or it will restrict their motion. Take the yarn through the stitch once or twice more to secure the fringe, then knot and weave the yarn in on the wrong side (WS) of the fabric.

Beaded Fringe Purse

What young lady wouldn't adore this little purse! It's the perfect accessory for a new spring dress.

This is a quick and easy knitting project. The beaded fringes are simple to make and not too time-consuming either.

Easy

FINISHED MEASUREMENTS
Approx 6½" x 6½"

MATERIALS
- Berroco Suede (100% nylon, 120 yds/111 m, 1.75 oz/50 g)
  2 balls #3755 Wyatt Earp (A)
  1 ball each #3753 Belle Star (B), #3754 Annie Oakley (C), and #3789 Nelly Belle (D)
- Approx 1100 size 11/0 Japanese seed beads. Sample knit with #11-574 silver lined lilac alabaster (2 tubes) from Caravan Beads.
- Three 6 mm round beads. Sample knit with 2 purple and 1 turquoise from Caravan Beads.
- Two 5" round purse handles. Sample handles from Judi & Co.
- Size 8 (5 mm) knitting needles, or size needed to obtain gauge.
- Size E/4(3.5mm) crochet hook (for edging and covering handles)
- Beading needle
- Beading thread to match bead and yarn
- Tapestry needle

GAUGE
With size 8 (5 mm) needles in St st, 19 sts and 28 rows in St st = 4"/10 cm.
To save time, take time to check gauge.

PATTERN STITCH
Stockinette Stitch (St st)
Knit on RS rows, purl on WS rows.

PATTERN NOTES
- Purse front, bottom, and back are constructed in 1 piece, then attached to side gussets.
- Stitch count includes 2 sts for selvedge, which is not included in measurements.
- When working Color Block pat, use Intarsia technique.
- Inc 1 by knitting (or purling) into the front and back of st.

INSTRUCTIONS

FRONT
With A, cast on 20 sts.

HEM FOR HANDLE
Beg with a RS row, work in St st for approx ¾", ending with a WS row.

Next Row (Inc Row): K1, inc 1, knit to last 2 sts, inc 1, k1—22 sts.

Cont in St st, and inc in this manner every row 5 times more—32 sts.

Cont even until piece measures approx 4¼" from beg, ending with a WS row.

Cut A.

SET UP COLOR BLOCK PAT
Next Row (RS): Join B and k first 11 sts, join C and k across next 10 sts, join D and k across rem 11 sts.

Cont working color blocks as est. for approx 2", ending with a WS row. Cut all 3 colors.

Join A and cont even in St st for approx 1". Front completed.

BOTTOM
Tie marker at beg and end of next row to indicate beg of purse bottom.

Work even in St st until bottom measures approx 2", ending with a WS row. Tie another marker at beg and end of last row to indicate end of purse bottom.

BACK
With A, work even until back measures same as front from end of shaping to beg of bottom (approx 5½" from end of bottom), ending with a WS row.

Next Row (Dec Row) (RS): K1, ssk, knit to last 3 sts, k2tog, k1—30 sts.

Next Row (Dec Row) (WS): P1, p2tog, purl to last 3 sts, ssp, p1—28 sts.

Rep last 2 rows twice more—20 sts.

HEM FOR HANDLE
Cont even in St st for approx ¾", ending with a WS row. Bind off.

SIDE GUSSET (MAKE 2)
With A, cast on 10 sts.

Beg with a RS row, work 8 rows in St st.

Next Row (Dec Row) (RS): K1, ssk, knit to last 3 sts, k2tog, k1—8 sts.

Rep Dec Row every 10th row 3 times—2 sts. Bind off.

FINISHING
Sew cast on edge of each gusset to side edges of bottom between markers. Fold front of purse up and sew to side of each gusset. Rep for back.

With crochet hook and A, work a slip stitch across shaped edge on each side.

Weave in yarn ends.

GLOSSARY OF TERMS AND TECHNIQUES

CABLES

Cables are made by taking a group of stitches and placing them on a cable needle, holding the cable needle either to the back or to the front of the work, working the next group of stitches, then working the first group of stitches from the cable needle.

If you hold the cable needle to the back of the work, the cable will twist to the right.

If the cable needle is held to the front of the work, the cable will twist to the left.

EMBROIDERY
Bullion Stitch

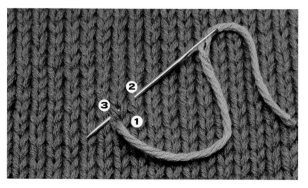

1. Thread needle with yarn or thread and bring up at 1. Take needle down at 2, and up again at 3, but do not pull yarn through fabric.

2. Wind yarn around needle 6–10 times (depending on size of stitch desired) to form a coil.

3. Then, holding yarn taut, gently pull needle through fabric and coil.

4. Take needle down a short distance from 3 to shape coil.

Basic Stem Stitch

Thread needle with yarn and working from right to left, bring needle up at 1. Take needle down at 2 and up again a half stitch back at 3. Repeat this sequence, working at a slight angle across area to be outlined.

FELTING

As with any project, you should knit a gauge swatch using the stitch pattern indicated. Make a note of the total measurements, and then felt it to get your felted gauge. This will also help determine the amount of felting time necessary to achieve the size and look you desire.

Place piece in a zippered pillow protector to protect your washer from yarn fibers that accumulate during the felting process, and place in washer. Set the machine for the smallest load size and hot water setting. To achieve the best results, you want a strong agitation, so add an old pair of blue jeans to make the load a bit heavier. Add a small amount, a teaspoon or less, of a clear liquid dishwashing soap, start your washer and timer. Felting can take place instantly . . . or not, so be vigilant. In approximately 4 to 5 minutes, stop the washer to check the progress of the felting. Remove the piece from the bag, taking care not to burn yourself, squeeze the water out, stretch this way and that, and check the size. Repeat every 4 to 5 minutes, resetting the machine to agitate until the piece is the desired size; DO NOT allow to drain and spin. Remove the now felted piece from its bag and rinse under lukewarm water from your sink faucet, until water runs clear. Squeeze out excess water by rolling in a towel.

Shape your piece, making sure the edges are straight and even. When you have achieved the desired size and look, leave the pieces to dry in an airy place, away from the sun and direct heat. DO NOT dry in a clothes dryer. It may take several hours, or a day or two for the pieces to dry completely.

POM-POMS

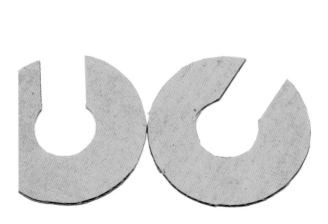

1. Cut out two cardboard circles in the size specified in the pattern for the pom-pom. Cut a hole approximately ½" in diameter in the center of each circle.

2. Thread tapestry needle with a long doubled length of yarn (thread more yarn as needed). Holding both circles together, insert needle through the center hole, over the outside edge, and then through the circle again until circle is completely covered and the center hole is filled. Carefully insert scissor blades between circles and cut around.

3. Cut two 12" strands of yarn and slip them between the circles, overlapping yarn ends two or three times.

4. Pull tightly and tie into a firm knot to prevent knot from slipping. Remove cardboard pieces. Roll pom-pom between your hands to fluff out. Trim evenly, leaving the tying ends for attaching pom-pom to your project.

SIMPLE FRINGE

*For each fringe, cut enough strands of yarn for half of the desired fullness of fringe and twice the desired length of fringe. Fold the strands in half, insert a crochet hook from back to front through the stitch, and pull the fold through to the back. Pull the ends through the fold, and pull to tighten. Repeat from * for each fringe. Trim fringe edges neatly to desired length.

TWISTED CORD

1. Cut strands of each yarn indicated in pattern approximately three times the desired length and knot them together about 1" from each end. Tie one end to a hook or door handle. Insert a pencil or knitting needle through the other end and twist the strands clockwise until yarn is tightly twisted.

2. Keeping the strands taut, fold the cord in half, allowing the two cords to twist upon themselves.

KNITTING ABBREVIATIONS

approx	approximately	RH	right-hand	WS	wrong side
beg	begin(ning)	rnd	round	wyib	bring yarn back between needles to the back of work
cm	centimeter	RS	right side (that is, public side)		
cn	cable needle	sc	single crochet	wyif	bring yarn forward between needles to the front of work
cont	continue(ing)	selv st	selvage stitch		
dec	decrease	skp	slip 1 stitch knitwise from left-hand needle to right-hand needle; knit next stitch, then pass the slipped stitch over the stitch just knit, then off needle. This is a left-leaning decrease.	yd(s)	yard(s)
dpn(s)	double pointed needle(s)			yo	yarn-over. Bring yarn forward between needles, then over right-hand needle into position to work the next stitch.
est	established				
g	gram(s)				
inc	increase				
k	knit				
k1-tbl	knit 1 stitch through the back loop				
k2tog	knit 2 stitches together as one, decreasing 1 stitch. This is a right-leaning decrease.	sk2p	slip 1 stitch knitwise, knit next 2 stitches together, then pass the slipped stitch over and off needle	*	repeat instructions after or between asterisks across row or round as instructed
k3tog	knit 3 stitches together as one, decreasing 2 stitches	sl st	slip stitch(es) as instructed	[ ]	repeat instructions within brackets as instructed
LH	left-hand	ssk	slip 2 stitches knitwise one at a time from left-hand needle to right-hand needle; insert left-hand needle through fronts of these stitches and knit them together as one. This is a left-leaning decrease.		
m	meter(s)				
M1	make 1 increase. Increase by inserting left-hand needle under horizontal strand between stitch just worked and next stitch; knit strand through the back.				
mm	millimeter(s)				
mult	multiple	ssp	slip next 2 stitches one at a time as if to knit; pass stitches back to left-hand needle and p2tog-tbl	BK1	knit 1 bead through a knit stitch
oz	ounce				
p	purl	st(s)	stitch(es)	BP1	purl 1 bead through a purl stitch
p1-tbl	purl 1 stitch through the back loop	s2kp2	slip 2 stitches together knitwise from left-hand needle to right-hand needle, knit next stitch, then pass the 2 slip stitches over the stitch just knit and off the needle.	SBU	slide bead up
p2tog-tbl	purl 2 stitches together as one, decreasing 1 stitch. This is a left-leaning decrease.				
pat(s)	pattern(s)				
pm	place marker(s)	tog	together		
rem	remain(ing)				
rep	repeat(s)				

KNIT WITH BEADS ABBREVIATIONS

SOURCES FOR MATERIALS

My sincere gratitude to the following suppliers, who generously provided materials for the projects in this book.

YARNS

These companies sell wholesale only. Please contact them to locate yarn shops and craft stores in your area that retail their products.

Berroco, Inc.
P.O. Box 367
114 Elmdale Road
Uxbridge, MA 01569
(508) 278-2527
www.berroco.com

Classic Elite Yarns, Inc.
122 Western Avenue
Lowell, MA 01851
(978) 453-2837
www.classiceliteyarns.com

Coats & Clark
Consumer Services
P.O. Box 12229
Greenville, SC 29612-0229
(800) 648-1479
www.coatsandclark.com

Green Mountain Spinnery
P.O. Box 568
Putney, VT 05346
(800) 321-9665
www.spinnery.com

JCA Crafts, Inc.
(Reynolds Signature)
35 Scales Lane
Townsend, MA 01469
(978) 597-8794
www.jcacrafts.com

Lion Brand Yarn Company
34 West 15th Street
New York, NY 10011
(212) 243-8995
www.lionbrand.com

Lorna's Laces
4229 North Honore Street
Chicago, IL 60613
(773) 935-3803
www.lornaslaces.net

Mountain Colors
P.O. Box 156
Corvallis, MT 59828
(406) 961-1900
www.mountaincolors.com

Muench Yarns
(GGH and GGH Wollywasch)
1323 Scott Street
Petaluma,CA 94954
(800) 733-9276
www.muenchyarns.com

Plymouth Yarn Company, Inc.
P.O. Box 28
Bristol, PA 19007
(215) 788-0459
www.plymouthyarn.com

BEADS

Lyden Enterprises, Home of
The Beadwrangler
228 N Sun Court
Tampa, FL 33613
(888) 235-0375
www.7beads.com
www.beadwrangler.com

Beads World, Inc.
1384 Broadway
New York, NY 10018
(212) 302-1199
www.beadsworldusa.com

Caravan Beads
326-A Nutt Street
Wilmington, NC 28401
(910) 343-0500
caravanbeads@bellsouth.net

BIBLIOGRAPHY

Allen, Pam, and Ann Budd. *Wrap Style.* Loveland, CO: Interweave Press, 2005.

Chin, Lily M. *Knit And Crochet with Beads.* Loveland, CO: Interweave Press, 2004.

Davis, Jane. *Knitting with Beads.* New York: Lark Books, 2003.

Durant, Judith, and Jean Campbell. *The New Beader's Companion.* Loveland, CO: Interweave Press, 2005.

Epstein, Nicky. *Knitting over the Edge.* New York: Sixth & Spring Books, 2005.

Hiatt, June Hemmons. *The Principles of Knitting.* New York: Simon and Schuster, 1988.

Miser, Lorna. *Knit & Fused Purses.* Berne, IN: American School of Needlework, 2005.

Rush, Hélène. *The Knitter's Design Sourcebook.* Camden, ME: Down East Books, 1991.

Stanley, Montse. *The Reader's Digest Knitter's Handbook* Pleasantville, NY: Reader's Digest, 1993.

Thomas, Mary. *Mary Thomas's Knitting Book.* London: Hodder and Stoughton, Ltd., 1943. Reprint. New York: Fireside, 2002.

Vogue Knitting Magazine, Editors of. *Vogue Knitting: The Ultimate Knitting Book.* New York: Pantheon Books, 1989.

Walker, Barbara G. *A Treasury of Knitting Patterns.* Pittsville, WI: Schoolhouse Press, 1998.

———. *A Second Treasury of Knitting Patterns.* Pittsville, WI: Schoolhouse Press, 1998.

Wiseman, Nancie M. *The Knitter's Book of Finishing Techniques.* Woodinville, WA: Martingale & Company, 2002.

Cartwright's Sequins
11108 N Hwy 348
Mountainburg, AR 72946
www.ccartwright.com

Wichelt Imports/Mill Hill
N162 Hwy 35
Stoddard, WI 54658
www.wichelt.com
www.millhill.com

NOTIONS

Susan Bates
(steel crochet hooks)
Distributed by Coats & Clark
See Coats & Clark

Judi & Co.
(round purse handles)
(631) 499-8480
www.judiandco.com

INDEX